CONTENTS

PROBLEM SOLVING

PROBLEM SOLVING

A HANDBOOK FOR TEACHERS

Stephen Krulik

Jesse A. Rudnick

Temple University

Allyn and Bacon, Inc.

Boston, London, Sydney, Toronto

Library of Congress Cataloging in Publication Data

Krulik, Stephen.
  Problem solving.

  Bibliography: p.
  1. Problem solving. I. Rudnick, Jesse A., joint author. II. Title.
QA63.K78   153.4'3   79-18817
ISBN 0-205-06847-2

Managing Editor: Robert Roen
Series Editor: David Pallai
Designer: Paula Carroll

Printed in the United States of America.

10 9 8 7 6 5 4 3 2   85 84 83 82 81 80

PREFACE

This book is designed to help you—whether you are a novice or an experienced classroom teacher—to teach *problem solving*. Ever since mathematics has been considered a school subject, the teaching of problem solving has been an enigma to mathematics teachers at all levels, whose frustrating efforts to teach students to become better problem solvers seem to have had little effect.

A major portion of the book is devoted to activities and carefully discussed non-routine problems which your students will find interesting as they gain valuable experience in problem solving. The activities and problems have been gleaned from a variety of sources, and have been classroom-tested at many levels by practicing teachers. We believe that this is the first time such an expansive set of problems has appeared in a single resource.

Ideologically we support the position paper of the National Council of Supervisors of Mathematics that classifies problem solving as a basic skill. However, we suggest that it is more than a single skill; rather, it is a group of several discreet skills. Thus in the chapter on pedagogy the subskills of problem solving are enumerated and then integrated into a teachable process. The chapter is highlighted by a flowchart which guides students through this vital process. Although there are many publications that deal with the problem-solving process, we believe that this is the first one that focuses on these subskills.

We are confident that this book will prove to be a valuable asset in your efforts to teach problem solving.

S.K. and J.R.

CHAPTER I

An Introduction to Problem Solving

WHAT IS A PROBLEM?

A major difficulty in discussing problem solving seems to be a lack of any clear-cut agreement as to what constitutes a "problem." A problem is a situation, quantitative or otherwise, that confronts an individual or group of individuals, that requires resolution, and for which the individual sees no apparent or obvious means or path to obtaining the solution. As people develop mathematically, what were problems initially are reduced to routine exercises. What may be a problem for one person may be an exercise for another, or of no interest to yet another.

We accept the principle that a problem must be perceived as such by a student, regardless of the reason, in order to be considered a problem by him or her. Thus a problem must satisfy the following three criteria, illustrated in Figure I-I.

1. *Acceptance:* The individual accepts the problem. There is a personal involvement which may be due to any of a variety of reasons, including internal motivation, external motivation (peer, parent, and/or teacher pressure), or simply the desire to experience the enjoyment of solving a problem.
2. *Blockage:* The individual's initial attempts at solution are fruitless. His or her habitual responses and patterns of attack do not work.
3. *Exploration:* The personal involvement identified in (1) forces the individual to explore new methods of attack.

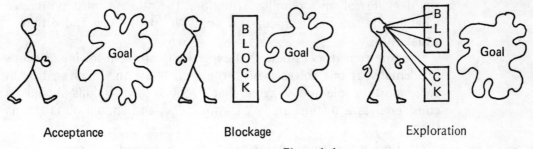

Acceptance　　　　　Blockage　　　　　Exploration

Figure 1-1

The existence of a problem implies that the individual is confronted by something he or she does not recognize, and to which he or she cannot merely apply a model. A problem will no longer be considered a problem once it can easily be solved by algorithms that have been previously learned.

A word about routine (verbal, textbook) problems: While most mathematics textbooks contain sections labeled "verbal problems," not all are really problems. In many cases, a model solution has already been presented in class by the teacher. The student merely applies this

3

model to the series of similar "problems" in order to solve them. Essentially the student is learning an algorithm—a technique that applies to a single class of "problems" and that guarantees success if mechanical errors are avoided. Few of these so-called problems require higher-order thought by the students. Yet the first time a student sees these "verbal problems," they may really be problems to him or her. Students do want to solve these exercises—mainly because the work has been assigned by the teacher, however, or because they need to obtain a good grade in the course. And students may experience blockage and frustration.

We consider these "verbal problems" to be "exercises," or "routine problems." This is not to say that we advocate removing them from the curriculum. They do serve a purpose, and for this purpose they should be retained. They provide exposure to problem situations, practice in the use of the algorithm, and drill in the associated mathematical processes. However, a teacher should not think that students who have been solving these routine exercises through use of a carefully developed model or algorithm have been exposed to problem solving.

WHAT IS PROBLEM SOLVING?

Problem solving is a process. It is the means by which an individual uses previously acquired knowledge, skills, and understanding to satisfy the demands of an unfamiliar situation. The student must synthesize what he or she has learned, and apply it to the new and different situation.

Some educators assume that expertise in problem solving develops incidentally as one solves many problems. While this may be true in part, most people today agree that problem-solving skills should be considered as a distinct body of knowledge, and should be taught as such.

The knowledge of mathematics can be divided into several parts, two of which are (1) information and facts and (2) the ability to use information and facts. This ability to use information and facts is an essential part of the problem-solving process.

WHY TEACH PROBLEM SOLVING?

In dealing with the issue of why we should teach problem solving, we must first consider the larger question: Why teach mathematics? The majority of students will rarely use pure higher mathematics in their everyday lives, but they will be required to solve quantitative problems that they meet in their social and working day. In almost every instance these quantitative situations will appear as problems. Rarely if ever are people confronted by situations that can be handled readily by the use of an algorithm. For most people, mathematics *is* problem solving!

In spite of the obvious relationship between mathematics of the classroom and the quantitative situations in life, we know that children of all ages see little connection between what happens in school and what happens in real life. An emphasis on problem solving in the classroom can lessen the gap between the real world and the classroom world and thus set a positive mood in the classroom.

In many mathematics classes, students do not see any connections among the various ideas taught during the semester's course of study. Most regard each topic as a separate entity. Problems show the interconnections among mathematical ideas. They are never solved in a vacuum, but are related in some way to something seen before, to something learned earlier. Thus good problems can be used to review past mathematical ideas, as well as to sow seeds for ideas to be presented at a future time.

Problem solving is more exciting, more challenging, and more interesting to children than barren exercises. If we examine student performance in the classroom, we recognize the obvious fact that success leads to persistence and continuation of a task; failure leads to avoidance. It is this continuance that we constantly strive for in mathematics. The greater the involvement, the better the end product. Thus a carefully selected sequence of problem-solving activities that yield success will stimulate students, leading them to a more positive attitude toward mathematics in general, and problem solving in particular.

Finally, problem solving permits students to learn and to practice heuristic thinking. A careful selection of problems is a major vehicle by which we provide a "sharpening" of problem-solving skills and strategies so necessary in real life.

WHEN DO WE TEACH PROBLEM SOLVING?

Since the process of problem solving is a teachable skill, when do we teach it? What does it replace? Where does it fit into the day-to-day schedule?

Experiences in problem solving are always at hand. All other activities are subservient. Thus the teaching of problem solving should occur in virtually every class period. Discussion of problems, proposed solutions, methods of attacking problems, etc., should be considered at all times. Think how poorly students would perform in other skill areas,

5

such as fractions, if they were taught these skills in one or two weeks of concentrated work and then the skills were never used.

Naturally there will be times when studies of algorithmic skills and drill and practice sessions will be called for. These times will permit the delay necessary for the incubation period required by many problems, which need time to "set." By allowing time between problem-solving sessions, you permit students to become familiar with the problem-solving process slowly, and over a longer period of time.

The number of problems discussed in any one class session must, of necessity, be small. This is a natural outgrowth of the process of problem solving. The goals are a study of the problem-solving process and growth in using this process, rather than merely "covering material."

WHAT MAKES A GOOD PROBLEM SOLVER?

Although we cannot easily determine what it is that makes some students good problem solvers, there are certain common characteristics exhibited by good problem solvers. For one thing, a good problem solver has a *desire* to solve problems. Problems interest him or her; they offer a challenge. Much like climbers of Mt. Everest, problem solvers like to solve problems because they exist.

Problem solvers are extremely *perseverant* when solving problems. They are not easily discouraged when incorrect, or when a particular approach leads to a dead end. They go back and try new approaches again and again. They refuse to quit!

If one method of attacking a problem fails to yield a satisfactory solution, successful problem solvers try another. A variety of methods of attack are usually at their disposal. They will often try the opposite of what they have been doing in the hope that new information will occur to them. They will ask themselves many "What if . . ." questions, changing the problem as they proceed.

Good problem solvers show an ability to skip some of the steps in the solution process. They make connections quickly, notice irrelevant detail, and often require only a few examples in order to generalize. They often show a marked lack of concern about neatness while developing their solution process.

Above all, good problem solvers are not afraid to guess! They will make "educated guesses" at solutions, and then attempt to verify these guesses. They will gradually refine their guesses on the basis of what previous guesses show them, until they find a satisfactory solution. They rarely guess wildly, but use their own intuition to make carefully thought through guesses.

6

We would suggest that good problem solvers are students who hold conversations with themselves. They know what questions to ask themselves, and what to do with the answers they receive as they think through the problem.

WHAT MAKES A GOOD PROBLEM?

It should be apparent to the reader that we consider problems to be the basic medium of problem solving. Furthermore, problem solving is the basic skill of mathematics. It follows, then, that without "good" problems we could not have creative mathematics.

What constitutes a good problem? First of all, teachers should be aware that there are good problems in every branch of mathematics, that problems need not be word problems in order to be good problems, and that good problems can be found everywhere. What follows in this section are some characteristics of good mathematics problems, together with examples which illustrate these characteristics. Keep in mind that not every good problem need have all of these characteristics. Neither is it always possible to clearly identify which characteristics make a problem good for problem solving—in many cases the characteristics will overlap. However, a good problem should have some of these attributes.

1. The solution to the problem involves a distinct mathematical concept or skill.

Many problems appear to be non-mathematical in context, yet the solution to the problems involves basic mathematical principles. Perhaps a pattern can be found that the students recognize. Or some application of a basic skill may quickly solve the problem. In any case, there should be some basic mathematical skill and/or concept imbedded in the problem and its solution.

PROBLEM   The new school has exactly 1,000 lockers and exactly 1,000 students. On the first day of school, the students meet outside the building and agree on the following plan: The first student will enter the school and open all of the lockers. The second student will then enter the school and close every locker with an even number (2, 4, 6, 8, . . .). The third student will then "reverse" every third locker. That is, if the

7

locker is closed, he will open it; if the locker is open, he will close it. The fourth student will reverse every fourth locker, and so on until all 1,000 students in turn have entered the building and reversed the proper lockers. Which lockers will finally remain open?

Discussion   It seems rather futile to attempt this experiment with 1,000 lockers, so let's take a look at 20 lockers and 20 students and try to find a pattern.

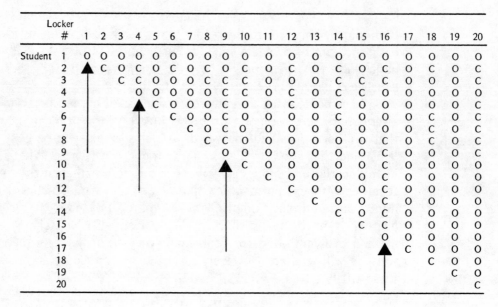

Figure 1-2

In our smaller illustration in Figure 1-2, the lockers with numbers 1, 4, 9, and 16 remain open, while all others are closed. Thus we conclude that those lockers with numbers that are perfect squares will remain open when the process has been completed by all 1,000 students. Notice that a locker "change" corresponds to a divisor of the locker number. An odd number of "changes" is required to leave a locker open. Which kinds of numbers have an odd number of divisors? Only the perfect squares!

PROBLEM   The Greens are having a party. The first time the doorbell rings, 1 guest enters. On the second ring, 3 guests enter. On the third ring, 5 guests enter, and so on. That is, on each successive ring, the entering group is 2 guests larger than the preceding group. How many guests will enter on the fifteenth ring? How many guests will be present after the fifteenth ring?

Discussion   Again, let's make a table and search for a pattern.

Ring number	People enter	Total present
1	1	1
2	3	4
3	5	9
4	7	16
5	9	25
6	11	36
·	·	·
·	·	·
·	·	·
n	$(2n-1)$	n^2

This means that on the fifteenth ring, $(2 \cdot 15 - 1)$ or 29 people will enter; a total of 225 people will have arrived after the fifteenth ring.

PROBLEM   There are 8 people in a room. Each person shakes hands with each of the other people once and only once. How many handshakes are there?

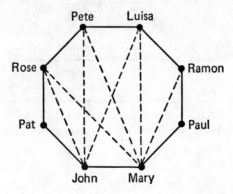

Figure 1-3

Discussion   This problem yields Figure 1-3, a geometric model of a convex octagon, where the vertices represent the people and the edges and diagonals represent the handshakes (only representative handshakes shown). Thus we are asking students to identify the number of diagonals plus the number of sides of a convex polygon. The answer is given by the mathematical formula

$$d = \frac{n(n-3)}{2} + n$$

This problem also illustrates the Fundamental Counting Principle. For elementary students, the problem should actually be acted out in the classroom.

2. The problem can be generalized or extended to a variety of situations.

A problem is not necessarily finished when a satisfactory solution has been found. The solution should suggest variations on parts of the original problem. The problem might be changed from a two-dimensional, plane-geometry problem to a three-space situation. Circles become spheres; rectangles become "boxes."

We might extend the problem to other cases. One variable might be held constant while another changes. We might generalize the problem from the specific case under scrutiny to a more general case. The shapes of a given figure might vary; the dimensions might change.

PROBLEM How many squares are there on a standard checkerboard?

Discussion This problem may be approached by considering the number of 1 X 1 squares, the number of 2 X 2 squares, the number of 3 X 3 squares, and so on up to the number of 8 X 8 squares. In tabular form these would be

Size of square	Number of squares
1 X 1	64
2 X 2	49
3 X 3	36
4 X 4	25
5 X 5	16
6 X 6	9
7 X 7	4
8 X 8	1
	Total: 204

Notice that this problem can be generalized to the number of squares on a 4 X 4 checkerboard, an n X n checkerboard, or an m X n rectangular checkerboard.

PROBLEM   Into how many different plane regions do *n* lines, no three of which are concurrent and none of which are parallel, separate the plane?

Discussion   This problem can be increased to three dimensions: "Into how many different space regions do *n* planes that do not intersect in a line and that are not parallel separate the space?"

We can also reduce the problem to one dimension: "Into how many different linear regions do *n* different points in a line separate the line?"

PROBLEM   In the "equation" *(he)*^{2} = *she*, the letters represent digits and the configurations represent numerals in base 10. Find replacements for the letters that make the statement true.

Discussion   If we were to select numerical values for *s*, *h*, and *e* at random, we would have approximately 1,000 possible combinations to test. However, we can impose some conditions about numbers and thus reduce our sample space radically:

1. *e*^{2} will produce the same units digit as does *e*.
   ∴ *e* must equal 0, 1, 5, or 6.
2. *(he)*^{2} will yield a three-digit number.
   ∴ *(he)*^{2} must lie between 100 and 1,000, or *(he)* must lie between 10 and 32.

Now we have reduced the possibilities to only 10. However, there is a third condition:

3. *(he)* appears on both sides of the equation, in both numerals.

Testing this condition yields the unique solution $(25)^2 = 625$.

PROBLEM   Find all rectangles with integral sides whose area and perimeter are numerically equal.

Discussion   Using the diagram in Figure 1–4, we express the problem mathematically.

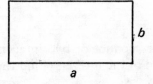

Figure 1–4

11

$$2a + 2b = ab$$

or

$$\frac{a + b}{ab} = \frac{1}{2}$$

A first solution is a 4 × 4 rectangle (square) whose perimeter and whose area both are 16. However, another set of values that satisfies the expressions is $a = 6$ and $b = 3$. This rectangle has a perimeter and an area of 18. These are the only two solutions to this problem.

In the previous problem, we saw that the equation we wanted to solve was

$$\frac{a + b}{ab} = \frac{1}{2}$$

This same equation can occur in extensions of the problem, as seen below.

PROBLEM   Find those pairs of integers that have 4 as their harmonic mean. (Note: The harmonic mean of two numbers is the reciprocal of the average of their reciprocals.)

Discussion   If we represent these integers by m and n, we obtain the relationship

$$\frac{\frac{1}{m} + \frac{1}{n}}{2} = \frac{1}{4}$$

$$\frac{1}{m} + \frac{1}{n} = \frac{1}{2}$$

$$\frac{m + n}{mn} = \frac{1}{2}$$

PROBLEM   The product of two integers is positive and equals twice the sum of the integers. Find the pair of integers.

Discussion   Represent the pair of integers by r and s. Then

An Introduction to Problem Solving

$$rs = 2(r + s)$$

$$1 = \frac{2(r + s)}{rs}$$

$$\frac{1}{2} = \frac{r + s}{rs}$$

These extensions, which lead to the same equation, are only one kind of problem extension. Still another kind of extension leads to further development of the original problem, as in the following case.

PROBLEM

For which positive integers a, b, and c will $\frac{1}{a} + \frac{1}{b} + \frac{1}{c} = 1$?

Discussion

An immediate solution is to let a, b, and c each equal 3. This yields the solution $1/3 + 1/3 + 1/3 = 1$. There is nothing in the statement of the original problem to preclude this. But while this solution does satisfy the problem, it clearly leaves us looking for more. A natural extension, then, is to add the condition that $a \neq b \neq c$. Now a solution is $a = 2, b = 3, c = 6$, since $1/2 + 1/3 + 1/6 = 1$.

A further extension might be to ask students for which positive integer n can we express n as the sum of the reciprocals of some number of different positive integers.

3. The problem lends itself to a variety of solutions.*

A problem can often be solved in many different ways. The problem-solving process may culminate in an algebraic solution, a geometric solution, or even a solution found through logical reasoning. It is of more value to the problem-solving process to solve one problem in four ways than to solve four problems, each in one way.

PROBLEM

Prove: If a point lies on one side of a triangle and is equally distant from the three vertices, then the triangle is a right triangle.

Discussion 1

Let P be the point on side AB of triangle ABC such that $AP = BP = CP$. Then label the angle measures x and y, using the properties of isosceles triangles APC and BPC. (See Figure 1-5.)

*This section was suggested by a paper by Dr. John F. Lucas, University of Wisconsin-Oshkosh, presented at the Ninth Annual Mathematics Symposium, Frostburg State College, Frostburg, Maryland, on April 28, 1978.

13

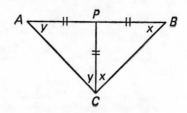

Figure 1-5

Now, since the sum of the measures of the angles of the triangle ABC equals 180°,

$$2x + 2y = 180$$
$$x + y = 90$$

which is the required proof.

Discussion 2 Triangle ABC can be inscribed in a circle, as in Figure 1-6. Since point P is equidistant from A, B, and C, then P must be the center of the circle.

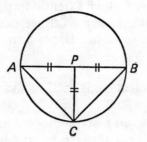

Figure 1-6

This makes APB a diameter of the circle, and an angle inscribed in a semicircle is a right angle.

Discussion 3 Extend segment CP its own length along ray CP to point D. Draw DA and DB. (See Figure 1-7.)

Now consider quadrilateral $CADB$. Since its diagonals bisect each other ($CP = PD$ by construction, $AP = PB$ by the given conditions), the quadrilateral must be a parallelogram. Furthermore, since the diagonals are congruent ($APB = DPC$), the parallelogram must be a rectangle. Hence angle C is a right angle.

14

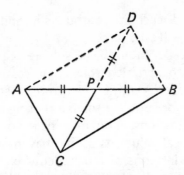

Figure 1-7

PROBLEM

A farmer has some pigs and some chickens. He finds that together they have 70 heads and 200 legs. How many pigs and how many chickens does he have?

Discussion 1

The problem can be solved algebraically by using two equations in two variables:

$$1p + 1c = 70 \text{ (heads)}$$
$$4p + 2c = 200 \text{ (legs)}$$
$$p = 30$$
$$c = 40$$

Discussion 2

A series of successive approximations will also enable students to find the solution:

All chickens (70)	140 legs
All pigs (70)	280 legs
20 pigs and 50 chickens	180 legs

Thus there must be more pigs:

30 pigs and 40 chickens	200 legs

Discussion 3

Use the idea of a one-to-one correspondence. All chickens stand on one leg, all pigs stand on hind legs. Thus the farmer will see 70 heads and 100 legs. The extra 30 legs must belong to the pigs, since the chickens have one leg per head. Thus there are 30 pigs and 40 chickens.

WHAT MAKES A GOOD TEACHER OF PROBLEM SOLVING?

All we have said about problems, problem solving, and problem solvers depends upon the teacher for implementation and fruition. Without an interested, energetic, enthusiastic, and involved guide or model, nothing positive will take place.

Success in problem solving requires a positive teacher attitude toward the problem-solving process itself. This means that teachers must prepare carefully for problem solving, and be aware of the opportunities for problem solving that present themselves in everyday classroom situations. You may have to modify a problem to assure its pedagogical value—its scope may have to be reduced, or the problem restated in terms of the students' experiences. Knowing your students helps you make these choices. Problems should be solved in class carefully, with the teacher allowing for and encouraging a wide variety of approaches, ideas, questions, solutions, and discussions. Teachers must be confident in class, and must exhibit the same enthusiasm for the problem-solving process that they wish to instill in their students.

Some teachers dislike problem solving because they have not had enough successful experiences in this area. Practice will provide these experiences. Teachers who encourage their students to solve problems, who make the students think, and who ask carefully worded questions (rather than merely giving answers) will provide their students with a rich problem-solving experience.

CHAPTER II

A
Workable
Set
of
Heuristics

WHAT ARE HEURISTICS?

We have defined an algorithm as a technique that applies to a single class of problems. An algorithm guarantees success if it is applied correctly and no arithmetic or mechanical errors are made. On the other hand, "heuristics" are creative guidelines that we use to help us solve problems. They are a set of suggestions; they cannot guarantee success. Then, too, they are far more general than an algorithm—they do not apply solely to a single class or type of problem.

In essence, heuristics are a general strategy, independent of a particular topic; suggestions that individuals can follow to help them approach a problem, understand the problem, and arrive at a solution to that problem. Techniques for solving specific problems should not be considered heuristics. For example, when solving a system of two algebraic equations in two variables, we try to eliminate one variable and reduce the system to a single equation with one variable. Even if we generalize this process to solving n equations in n variables by reducing the number of variables to $(n - 1)$ and the number of equations to $(n - 1)$, we are still talking about an algorithm rather than a heuristic. It is only relevant for working with n equations in n variables. Successful problem solvers have found that, in solving a wide variety of problems, they pursue many of the same steps. Whether we follow the heuristics developed by Polya or some other set of heuristics is not important; what is important is that our students be equipped with some set of carefully developed heuristics, and that they develop the habit of applying these heuristics in problem-solving situations.

It is apparent that simply providing students with a set of heuristics to follow would be of little value. There is quite a difference between understanding a strategy on an intellectual plane (recognizing and describing it) and being able to actually apply the strategy. Thus we must do more than merely hand the heuristics to the students—rather, instruction must focus on the thinking that the problem solver goes through as he or she considers a problem. It is the process—not the answer—that is problem solving.

Applying heuristics is a difficult skill in itself. We must spend time showing students how (and when) to use each of the heuristics—a prescriptive approach rather than merely a descriptive one. Then we must constantly use and refer to the heuristics as our students solve problems.

A SET OF HEURISTICS TO USE

Although there are as many sets of heuristics as there are problem solvers, let's look at one such set which has worked with students in classrooms at various levels. Keep in mind that not all of the heuristic steps need to be considered in every problem.

1. Read

1a. Note key words.
1b. Get to know the problem setting.
1c. What is being asked for?
1d. Restate the problem in your own words.

PROBLEM   What is the lowest common denominator for the two fractions 1/3 and 1/12?

Discussion   Notice that the key word here is "lowest." We could find *a* common denominator easily enough by multiplying 12 × 3 to get 36. But that is not the lowest common denominator.

PROBLEM   Jeff weighs 160 pounds. His sister Nancy weighs 108 pounds. Scott weighs 26 pounds more than Nancy. What is the average weight of all three people?

Discussion   Here the key words are "more than" and "average." Words such as "more than," "less than," "subtracted from," etc., are often overlooked by students.

2. Explore

2a. Draw a diagram, or construct a model.
2b. Make a chart. Record the data.
2c. Look for patterns.

PROBLEM   A log is cut into 4 pieces in 9 seconds. At the same rate, how long would it take to cut the log into 5 pieces?

Discussion   Notice the key phrase "at the same rate."
    In many cases, students react to this problem as an exercise in proportion:

$$\frac{4}{9} = \frac{5}{x}$$

    If they draw a diagram, as in Figure 2–1, they quickly see that the solution process should focus on the number of cuts needed to get the required number of pieces, rather than on the actual number of pieces.

Figure 2-1

Once the diagram has been interpreted, students should realize that they do not need proportions. They see that 3 cuts produced 4 pieces, and thus they need 4 cuts to produce 5 pieces. Since 3 cuts were made in 9 seconds, each cut required 3 seconds. Therefore the necessary 4 cuts will require 12 seconds.

PROBLEM   A farmer wishes to purchase a piece of land that is adjacent to his farm. The real estate agent tells him that the plot is triangular in shape, with sides of 20, 75, and 45 meters. This land will cost only $5.58 a square meter. How much should the farmer pay for the piece of land?

Discussion   The problem can be solved in a geometry class by using Heron's formula,

$$A = \sqrt{s(s-a)(s-b)(s-c)}$$

(where s equals half the perimeter). If the students draw a diagram, however, as in Figure 2-2, it becomes readily apparent that there is no such triangle, since the sum of two of the sides is not greater than the third side (45 + 20 < 75).

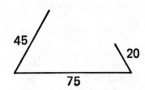

Figure 2-2

PROBLEM   Claire drove from Philadelphia to Brooklyn, then to Manhattan, then to Scarsdale. She returned over the same route.

From Philadelphia to Brooklyn is 93 miles. From Brooklyn to Manhattan is 11 miles. The trip from Scarsdale to Philadelphia was 131 miles. What is the distance between Manhattan and Scarsdale?

Discussion   While the problem sounds cumbersome, confusing, and full of excess data, it can be simplified by the use of a diagram, as in Figure 2-3.

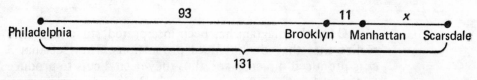

Figure 2-3

$$
\begin{array}{ll}
\text{Philadelphia to Brooklyn} = & 93 \\
\text{Brooklyn to Manhattan} \ \ = & 11 \\
\underline{\text{Manhattan to Scarsdale} \ \ = \ \ x} \\
\qquad\qquad\qquad 131 \qquad\quad = 104 + x
\end{array}
$$

PROBLEM   The 7 and 8 keys on my calculator don't work. How might I find the sum of 274 + 882 + 1,028?

Discussion   We can approach this problem by recording the data in column form:

$$
\begin{array}{rl}
274 = & 264 + \ \ 10 \\
882 = & 662 + 220 \\
1,028 = & 1,020 + \ \ \ 6 + 2
\end{array}
$$

Once students see how to regroup the first number, the pattern follows quickly.

PROBLEM   Find the next three numbers in the sequence 2, 3, 5, 8, 12.

Discussion   We record these numbers in a row as in Figure 2-4, and examine the differences between successive terms.

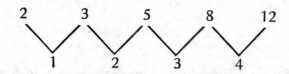

Figure 2-4

The natural numbers give the first differences, and we can find the next three terms (17, 23, 30) quite easily. (There are other ways to examine this sequence. See problem 8 in Section B.)

PROBLEM   Into how many segments do *n* points divide a given line segment?

Discussion   First draw a diagram, as in Figure 2-5.

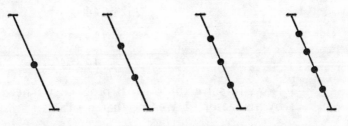

Figure 2-5

Then organize the data by completing a table. Look for a pattern.

Number of points	1	2	3	4	•	•	•	*n*
Number of segments	2	3	4	5	•	•	•	$(n+1)$

3. Select a strategy

3a. Experiment.
3b. Look for a simpler problem.
3c. Conjecture/guess.
3d. Form a tentative hypothesis.
3e. Assume a solution.

PROBLEM   The sides of a rectangle are 60 and 144. How long is the diagonal of the rectangle?

Discussion   The problem suggests the use of the Pythagorean Theorem. However, the numbers are extremely large. A simpler problem would be a problem with smaller numbers. In this case, we can examine a rectangle similar to the original but with each linear dimension divided by 12. (See Figure 2-6.)

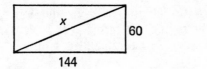

Figure 2-6

Now we apply the Pythagorean Theorem to the second situation:

$$5^2 + 12^2 = y^2$$
$$25^2 + 144 = y^2$$
$$169 = y^2$$
$$13 = y$$

Now, to solve the original problem we need only multiply by the factor 12. We find that $x = 156$.

The following problem can be solved through the use of a simpler problem that is a model of the original problem but contains fewer cases.

PROBLEM   A Polaris Commuter has seats for 108 passengers. On a flight to Memphis, there was 1 empty seat for every 2 passengers actually on board. How many passengers were on the flight?

Discussion   A simpler problem would be one that considered a plane with seats for 12 passengers.

E   X   X
E   X   X
E   X   X
E   X   X

Empty	People	Total
1	2	3
2	4	6
3	6	9
4	8	12

The pattern revealed by the table leads to

$$x + 2x = 108$$

PROBLEM   How many different ways can you add four odd natural numbers and get 10 as the sum?

Discussion   Students should remember that "sum" implies addition. They should ask questions such as "How many numbers must I add?" and "Why isn't 4 + 2 + 2 + 2 a solution?"
            Students will try different sets of numbers to see if they add up to 10. Keep guessing and checking until all the ways have been found. Keeping the results in an organized table will help. Notice that 7 + 1 + 1 + 1 is the same as 1 + 1 + 1 + 7 is the same as 1 + 7 + 1 + 1 and so on. These all count as one way.

PROBLEM   There are three natural numbers that are less than one thousand which are both perfect squares and perfect cubes. Find these three numbers.

Discussion   First students should reread the problem several times to be certain that they understand the conditions of the problem. They might even be able to guess the first numbers that satisfy the conditions, namely 1 and 64. They might then make a list of the numbers that are perfect squares and a list of the numbers that are perfect cubes. They then examine the lists to find the numbers that appear on both. Preparing the lists provides an excellent opportunity to use the hand-held minicalculator. (The third number is 729.)

PROBLEM   On a table there are three boxes of lima beans. The boxes are labeled A, B, and C. The sum of the numbers of lima beans in A and B is 195. The difference between the numbers of lima beans in B and C is 150. The sum of the numbers of beans in A and C is 345. The difference between the numbers of beans in A and C is 25. How many lima beans are there in each box?

Discussion   Students should notice that the last two sentences refer to the number of lima beans in both A and C. Using this information, students might make a guess as to the correct answers. They should then check their guesses. If these guesses do not work, other guesses should be made and checked. (A contains 185 beans; B contains 10 beans; C contains 160 beans. Or A contains 160 beans; B contains 35 beans; C contains 185 beans).

4. Solve

4a. Carry through your strategy.

Once a method of attack has been selected, the students should apply the method to the problem—by going through the process and arriving at an answer.

PROBLEM A basketball player can dribble a ball 18 times in 10 seconds; how many dribbles can she do in 1 minute? How long does it take to do 63 dribbles?

Discussion Students can construct a table to solve this problem. Some students may make a table that only carries the problem out through 30 seconds; others will carry the table all the way out to 60 seconds.

Seconds	10	20	30	40	50	60
Dribbles	18	36	54	72	90	108

It is interesting to note that the problem does not state that the rate is constant. Some students may wish to discuss the fact that, as time passes, the ballplayer might become tired and do fewer dribbles in each time period.

Some simple interpolation is required to find the answer to the second part of the problem. Use a proportion.

5. Review and extend.

5a. Verify your answer.
5b. Look for interesting variations on the original problem.

PROBLEM Find the length of 1 school desk if the sum of the lengths of 4 such desks is 56 feet.

Discussion Notice that in this problem the word "sum" does not ensure that the problem will be solved by addition.

$$4x = 56$$

$$x = 14$$

The answer appears to be 14 feet. Are the units correct? Does the method appear to yield a correct solution? Does the answer "make sense"? (After all, 14 feet is rather a large desk.) Why or why not?

PROBLEM   Find the weight of 1 liter of wine if 4 liters of wine weigh 1,260 grams.

Discussion   Although the word "sum" does not appear in the problem and the problem is not about lengths, the method of solution is exactly the same as in the previous problem. Note that this is a variation of the previous problem.

PROBLEM   Figure 2-7 is an array of 17 toothpicks forming 6 squares. By removing exactly 6 of the toothpicks, leave exactly 2 squares.

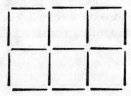

Figure 2-7

Discussion   After the thought that "It can't be done!" the initial student reaction is to think in terms of squares of the same size. With this restriction, they are right—it can't be done. However, if we are not restricted to squares of the same size (and nothing in the problem tells us we are so restricted), a solution is as depicted in Figure 2-8.

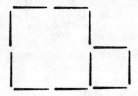

Figure 2-8

Notice that "restrictions" are usually something that is self-imposed. As a variation of this kind of problem, an extension that students find interesting, you might try the following one.

PROBLEM   Jeff and Barbara are both good chess players. They have completed 5 games, and each has won the same number of games. There were no ties. How might this have been done?

Discussion   Again, the same kind of self-imposed restriction leads students to think that the two players, Barbara and Jeff, played *against each other.* Yet there is no such restriction. The problem is easily solved if we remove this self-imposed restriction and realize that they played their 5 games against different opponents.

PROBLEM

Mark has accepted a new job with an unusual pay scale. He will receive $1 the first week, $2 the second week, $4 the third week, and so on. Each week the salary will be twice that of the previous week. How much money will Mark have earned after 4 weeks? After 8 weeks? After 20 weeks?

Discussion

We can solve this problem by considering what happens at the end of 1 week, 2 weeks, 3 weeks, etc., and arranging the data in tabular form.

Week	Weekly salary	Total earned
1	$1	$1
2	$2	$3 (1 + 2)
3	$4	$7 (1 + 2 + 4)
4	$8	$15 (1 + 2 + 4 + 8)

Notice that the weekly salary can be expressed as a power of 2, namely $2^{(n-1)}$. The total salary can be expressed in either of two ways:

$$2^0 + 2^1 + 2^2 + 2^3 + 2^4 + \ldots + 2^{(n-1)}$$

or

$$2^n - 1$$

Thus the amount Mark earns after 4 weeks will be $2^4 - 1$, or $15. The amount earned after 8 weeks will be $2^8 - 1$, or $255. For the twentieth week, the amount will be $2^{20} - 1$, or $1,048,575.

The following problem is an interesting variation of this problem involving rapid increases through the doubling process.

PROBLEM

Take a sheet of paper and tear it in half. Place the 2 pieces of paper atop one another, and tear them in half. This gives 4 pieces of paper. Place them on top of one another, and tear them in half again. Imagine continuing this process through 20 such tears. How many sheets are now in the pile of paper? If each sheet of paper is .001 inches thick, how high is the pile of paper?

Discussion   After 1 tear, the pile is 2 layers thick. After 2 tears, it is 4 layers thick. After n such tears, the pile will be 2^n layers thick. After 20 such tears, the pile will be 2^{20} or 1,048,576 layers thick. If the paper has a thickness of .001 inches, the pile will be about 87 feet (or 1,048 inches) high.

APPLYING THE HEURISTICS

Now that we have presented and illustrated a set of heuristics, let's look at some classroom experiences in problem solving, applying the heuristics.

PROBLEM   Twelve couples have been invited to a party. The couples will be seated at a series of small square card tables, placed end to end so as to form one large long table. How many of these small tables are needed to seat all 24 people?

Discussion   **1. Read.**

Note key words. Get to know the problem setting. What is being asked for? Restate the problem in your own words.

At first students tend to guess wildly, with no thought. The key words in the problem are "square tables" and "placed end to end," as well as "24 people."

2. Explore.

Draw a diagram.

Students should draw a picture of what the situation looks like for 1 table, for 2 tables, for 3 tables, etc. (See Figure 2–9.)

29

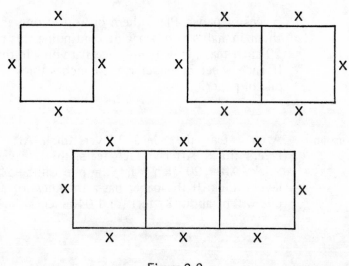

Figure 2-9

Make a chart. Record the data. Look for patterns.

Number of tables	1	2	3	4	•	•	•	n
Number of guests	4	6	8	10	•	•	•	24

There does seem to be a pattern here. As we add a table, the number of guests that can be seated is increased by 2.

3. Select a strategy.
Look for a simpler problem.

Suppose we limit the number of guests to a smaller number, say 16. Let's see if our pattern holds true. Extend the chart.

Number of tables	1	2	3	4	5	6	7
Number of guests	4	6	8	10	12	14	16

Conjecture. Form a tentative hypothesis.

Since the pattern seems to be holding true for 16 guests, we can continue to add 1 table for every 2 additional guests until we reach our required number of 24 guests. We thus add 4 additional tables for the additional guests (16 + 8 = 24). This is our hypothesis: it will take 11 tables to accommodate 24 guests.

4. Solve.
Carry through your strategy.
    One way to solve the problem is to continue the chart until we reach the required number of guests.

Number of tables	1	2	3	4	5	6	7	8	9	10	11
Number of guests	4	6	8	10	12	14	16	18	20	22	24

    This seems to satisfy our original hypothesis. We might also "prove the answer by placing 11 small squares (to represent the tables) in a row, end to end. Then we could actually count the places to be certain that the tables actually seat the 24 guests.

5. Review and extend.
    We might ask our students to develop a formula for seating any given number of guests *n*. This yields the expression

$$t = \frac{n-2}{2}$$

where *t* represents the number of tables.
    Or we might ask for a formula to determine how many guests we can seat, given the number of tables.

$$n = 2t + 2$$

or

$$n = 2(t + 1)$$

PROBLEM   What is the maximum number of regions into which *n* chords can divide a circle?

Discussion   **1. Read.**
Note key words. Get to know the problem setting. What is being asked for? Restate the problem in your own words.
    The key word in our problem is "maximum." This suggests that the placement of the chords will be important.

2. Explore.
Draw a diagram.
    First we will try parallel chords and intersecting chords

to see the effect these have on the number of regions. (See Figure 2-10.)

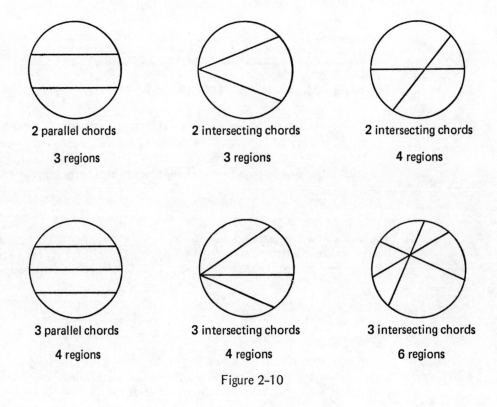

2 parallel chords

3 regions

2 intersecting chords

3 regions

2 intersecting chords

4 regions

3 parallel chords

4 regions

3 intersecting chords

4 regions

3 intersecting chords

6 regions

Figure 2-10

It is now apparent that parallel chords will not give a *maximum* number of regions, nor will chords that intersect on the circle. But what about non-concurrent chords? Suppose the chords we choose are neither parallel nor concurrent, as in Figure 2-11.

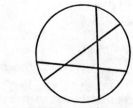

3 intersecting, non-concurrent chords

7 regions

Figure 2-11

This tells us that our chords should be neither parallel nor concurrent, nor intersecting on the circle.
Make a chart. Record the data. Look for patterns.
Let us prepare a chart to see if we can find any patterns.

Number of chords	Number of regions
1	2
2	4
3	7
4	11

3. Select a strategy.
Conjecture/guess. Form a tentative hypothesis.
Observe that as the number of chords is increased by 1 (linearly), the difference in the number of added regions is increased quadratically. Our hypothesis is that this pattern will continue.

Number of chords	Number of regions
1	2
2	4
3	7
4	11
5	16
6	22

4. Solve.
Carry through your strategy.
Let us find a formula that describes this pattern. Construct a table of differences.

Number of chords	Number of regions	First Differences	Second Differences
1	2		
		2	
2	4		1
		3	
3	7		1
		4	
4	11		1
		5	
5	16		1
		6	
6	22		

Since the second differences are constant, the relation is quadratic. The maximum number of regions (r) into which n chords will divide a circle is given by the formula

$$r = \frac{n^2 + n + 2}{2}$$

5. Review and extend.

Develop a similar procedure for the number of diagonals of an increasing n-gon.

The Pedagogy of Problem Solving

The problem-solving process suggests that some set of heuristics be jointly developed and used by the teacher and students. Whether this set is Polya's four-step heuristics, or the set suggested in Chapter 2, or some other set of seven, eight, or even more steps is not important. What is important is that the students develop an organized set of "questions" to ask themselves and that they constantly refer to them when they are confronted by a problem situation.

What can the teacher do to assist the students in achieving this important goal? In this chapter we will present methods that the teacher can employ in the classroom to assist students in the utilization of heuristics in their development of problem-solving skills. Activities are included for use with students.

1. Create an atmosphere of success.

The old adage "Nothing succeeds like success" holds true in the mathematics classroom. Remember: if a student refuses to even attempt to solve a problem, there can be no problem-solving activity. Choose the problems carefully. Begin with relatively simple problems so as to ensure a reasonable degree of success. If students are successful, they are likely to be "turned on" to problem solving, whereas repeated failure or constant frustration can have a devastating effect on motivation, attitude, and the desire to continue.

The breadth and depth of knowledge required, as well as the sequence of problems chosen, should be kept in mind as major criteria for developing suitable problem-solving situations. Consider the possibility of a series of brief, quickly done problems, each one leading to a more difficult problem, until the original problem-solving task has been completed. This procedure of breaking up a problem into a series of short steps will help those students with short attention spans to enjoy success and to become interested in progress toward the solution of problems.

PROBLEM   In a class, half of the students are boys. Six boys are present. One-fourth of the boys are present. How many students (boys and girls) are there in the entire class, when all students are present?

Discussion   Introduction of this problem might be followed by a series of brief questions. For instance:

1. How many boys are present?
2. If this is one-fourth of the boys on role, how many boys are on role?
3. What part of the whole class is boys?

37

Answering these short questions could easily lead the student to the solution of the original problem, namely 48 students.

Success means more than the correct answer. Becoming absorbed in a problem and making a sustained attempt at solution is also success.

2. Encourage your students to solve problems.

In order for students to become good problem solvers, they must be constantly exposed to and involved in problem solving. In teaching someone to swim, the "theory" can go just so far; eventually, the real ability to swim must come from actually swimming. It is the same way in problem solving. Students must solve problems! The teacher should try to find problems that are of interest to the students. Listen to them as they talk; they will often tell you about the things in which they are interested. (Problems derived from television and sports always generate enthusiasm among students.)

PROBLEM The weight of a $1 bill is 1 gram. A basketball player's salary is $1 million. The player insists on being paid in $1 bills. Could the player carry his salary in a suitcase? Suppose he decided to accept $20 bills instead?

Discussion Consider that the example concerns itself not only with weight, but also with volume (of the suitcase). Yet no dimensions have been given. ($1,000,000 = 1,000,000$ grams $= 1$ metric ton.)

PROBLEM Superman and Lothar are mortal enemies. Superman is about to enter Lothar's secret hideaway. Inside, Lothar has 5 "zap" guns, each of which can fire 3 kryptonite bullets at Superman. How many times can Lothar fire a kryptonite bullet at Superman?

Discussion Notice the similarity to the basic textbook problem "Jane wants to buy 3 oranges at 5¢ each. How much money does she need to buy the oranges?"

ACTIVITY Take several exercises from the students' textbook. Encourage the students to change the setting of the problem to one that is more interesting to them. Emphasize that the problem must contain the same data as the original.

Discussion One effect of this activity will be to force the students to decide what the problem is really all about. At the same time they will be engaged in creating problems similar to the original but more interesting to them.

Another way to encourage your students to solve problems is to stop occasionally in class in order to analyze what it is that you are doing and why the processes were undertaken in a particular manner. Focus the students' attention on the larger issue of a general strategy as well as on the specific details of the particular problem at hand. If difficulties arise, make yourself available to *help* students; do not solve the problem for them.

ACTIVITY Present students with problems that do not contain specific numbers. Ask them to discuss what operations are called for.
EXAMPLE: Jeff wants to buy a pen, a notebook, and an eraser for school. How can he be sure that he has sufficient money?
EXAMPLE: You know the age of an elephant in years and months. How many months old is the elephant?

Try to solve problems in more than one way. Doing this will increase the number of alternative approaches available to the students the next time they face a problem situation.

PROBLEM A, B, and C decide to play a game of cards. They agree on the following procedure: When a player loses a game, he or she will double the amount of money that each of the other players already has. First A loses a hand and doubles the amount of money that B and C each have. Then B loses a hand and doubles the amount of money that A and C each have. Then C loses a hand and doubles the amount of money that A and B each have. The three players then decide to quit, and they find that each player now has $8. Who was the biggest loser?

Discussion This problem can be solved in an algebra class by writing a series of 3 equations in 3 unknowns. Once this is done, the system of equations can be solved easily.
    An alternative approach might be to suggest to the class that they try to solve the problem by working backwards. This quickly yields the solution, and at an artistic, less mathematically sophisticated level. At the same time, it provides the students with an additional approach to problem solving (namely, working backwards).

A	Player B	C	
8	8	8	game 3
4	4	16	game 2
2	14	8	game 1
13	7	4	start

3. Teach students how to read the problem.

The basic heuristic in any heuristic system is to read the problem carefully. Yet students often overlook essential ideas and implications within the context of the problem. Since most problems in school are presented in written form, proper reading habits are essential.

ACTIVITY   It is important to alert your students to the fact that not all mathematics is read from left to right. The eye views simple expressions such as

$$\frac{3}{8} + \frac{4}{8} = \frac{7}{8}$$

in a variety of different directions, as shown by the following "arrow diagram":

$$\left|\frac{3}{8}\right| + \left|\frac{4}{8}\right| = \left|\frac{7}{8}\right|$$

Prepare a transparency containing several different mathematical expressions. Have students draw correct arrow diagrams for each one.

Many activities should be used to help students sharpen their ability to read critically and carefully for meaning. One such technique is to have the students underline or circle words that they consider to be key words in a problem. Discuss these words with the class. Have students indicate why they consider these particular words to be key words.

PROBLEM   If the length of the Loch Ness monster is 20 meters and half of its own length, how long is the monster?

Discussion   Some students will decide that the monster is 20 meters long plus half of 20 meters (10), or a total of 30 meters in length.

These students have overlooked the words "and half of its own length." Once these words have been carefully considered, students should interpret the problem to mean that the monster's full length is the sum of 20 meters and half the total length. Thus the monster is really divided into two equal halves. If the monster's full length is one of these halves plus 20 meters, then the 20 meters must represent the other half, and the full length of the monster is 40 meters. The same result can easily be found with the algebraic equation

$$x = 20 + \frac{x}{2}$$

where x is the total length of the Loch Ness monster

ACTIVITY Write a problem on a slip of paper. Have one student read the problem silently, put it away, and then relate the problem in his or her own words to the rest of the class. In this way, students often reveal whether they have found the facts that are really important to the solution of the problem, or whether they have missed the point entirely.

ACTIVITY Show a problem on a transparency on the overhead projector. After a short period of time, turn the projector off and have the class restate the problem in their own words.

ACTIVITY One way to encourage practice in reading mathematics problems slowly and for understanding is to mimeograph a page from a mathematics textbook, cut the page into pieces much like those of a jigsaw puzzle, and have the students put the page together again.

Since many words have a special meaning in the mathematics classroom which is different from the regular meaning, the class should discuss a list of such words together with their various meanings. (A beneficial project would be the compilation of a dictionary in which each word is defined mathematically and in other contexts.)

ACTIVITY Discuss the different meanings of the following words:

volume	chord	function	prime
root	difference	mean	times
count	element	power	

ACTIVITY   Duplicate a series of problems, leaving out every tenth word. Ask your students to try to fill in the blanks. (Note: As your students become more proficient in this skill, you can leave out every seventh word, every fifth word, etc.)

Finally, you can use problems at a low reading level for those students whose reading abilities are very weak.

ACTIVITY   Look at the toys in Figure 3-1.

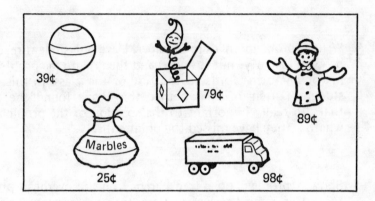

Figure 3-1

What sets of toys can you buy for $2?
Which toy is the most expensive?
Which two toys can you buy for less than $1?

These and similar activities available from the school's reading specialist will teach your students to read the problems more critically and to understand them better.

4. Involve your students in the problem.

Let the students be a part of the action. Involve them in the story. Have students actually perform as the problem dictates.

PROBLEM   How fast can you bounce a basketball? That is, how many times can you bounce the basketball in 1 minute?

PROBLEM   Can you roll a marble along the chalk tray in your classroom as quickly as you can run a distance of 100 yards?

Notice that these problems allow the students to actually get into the problem. They become a part of the story. Out come stopwatches, basketballs, marbles, and so on. The entire class becomes actively engaged in the problem-solving process.

PROBLEM   Three boys stood on a scale and put a nickel in the slot. The scale showed 390 pounds as their total weight. One boy stepped off the scale. It then showed 255 pounds. The second boy stepped off the scale, and it then showed 145 pounds. Find the weights of all three boys.

Discussion   In class, you could ask three boys to actually act out this problem. They might step back onto the "scale" to check their weights.

Using manipulable materials in problem solving is another way to enable your students to become active participants. If students must work directly with the materials to solve problems, they cannot just sit back and become spectators. The materials can easily be stored in shoeboxes or in large envelopes, along with a series of activity cards posing the problems.

PROBLEM   How many 3-rod trains can you make that are equal in length to 1 orange rod? (Cuisenaire Rods)

Discussion   Notice that this is the same problem as "How many different ways can you select 3 natural numbers such that their sum is 10?" Yet it involves the use of concrete materials.

PROBLEM   How many squares can you construct on a 4 × 4 geoboard? (Geoboard and rubber bands)

PROBLEM   Figure 3-2 contains pictures of 3 figures that were made with the 7 Tangram pieces. Try to make each one using all 7 pieces. Record your solution on paper. (Tangrams)

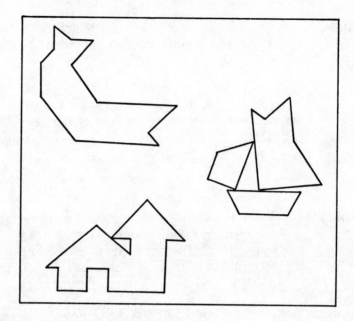

Figure 3-2

5. Require your students to create their own problems.

Considerable insight into the problem-solving process can be gained by having students make up their own problems. Given a stimulus, students at any age level will create good problems. Some ideas for these problems must be provided, however.

ACTIVITY   Show pictures that have been taken from old magazines, old textbooks, etc. Have the students make up their own numerical data and a story problem to fit each picture.

Discussion   This activity helps students learn to decide on numerical data that makes sense, for they must use realistic numbers in their problem designing. At the same time, this activity helps students to integrate mathematical problem solving with other subjects, such as social studies, language arts, and science.

Sharing problems that have been written by other students should be an integral part of your classroom procedure. The fact that the problems have been designed by classmates usually heightens interest in solving them. These problems may simply be variations of other problems that students have seen, or they may be entirely original creations.

Remember that not all of the problems need have a solution; it is the problem-solving process that is being stressed. In fact, it is often desireable to have students create problems with too much information or insufficient information. This is an interesting and worthwhile task, for when other students attempt to solve these problems, they usually find themselves heavily involved in determining the amount of information given.

PROBLEM   How much meat does a 100-pound lion eat in one week?

PROBLEM   Find the area of a parallelogram whose adjacent sides are 8 centimeters and 6 centimeters.

PROBLEM   Jan has 84 seashells in her collection. She decided to give 5 shells to each of 3 friends. How many shells did she give away?

In all cases above, the discussion of the sufficiency of information given in the problem is of more value than the answer.

Notice that problems that appear in textbooks often emphasize one particular skill or operation. On the other hand, student-generated problems frequently involve extraneous data and possibly more than one operation.

ACTIVITY   Ask your students to write a "menu problem." That is, given the following menu, write a problem about it.

Hot dog	.70
Hamburger	.85
Pizza (slice)	.50
Tuna sandwich	.95
Grilled cheese sandwich	.85
Apple	.25
Bananas	2 for .45
Milk (white)	.20
Milk (chocolate)	.25
Candy	2 for .35

6. Have your students work together in pairs or small groups.

Team problem solving and group brainstorming are viable techniques in the business world. Rarely does any one person solve major problems alone. While the final decisions do fall on one person, the group input helps the problem-solving process. A student's inability or refusal to help in the group process can be a direct hindrance to decision making. Thus the classroom teacher must provide guidance and practice in the particular skills involved in sharing ideas

The interaction provided by cooperating students will help them learn to modify one another's thinking, and to defend their own positions while considering the positions of other students. They will also learn to express their thoughts more clearly by the use of precise language, especially mathematical terminology—students will find it difficult to communicate with others unless they use language that every member of the group can agree upon.

The group may want to focus on a problem-solving situation as a series of motion-picture frames. The sequential nature of this image helps students decide what comes first, what comes second, and so on. With contributions from various members of the group, the class can develop a sequence of activities to solve the problem.

ACTIVITY   One technique that helps students to sharpen up group interaction is the following. When your students are all seated in their groups, place a set of totally unrelated objects in front of each group. (For example, a handful of popcorn, a lump of modeling clay, and a plastic cup.) Allow the group about ten minutes to decide what to do with these objects and then to act on their decision. After the time period has elapsed, ask each group to explain what they did with the objects and, if possible, why.

ACTIVITY   Students are divided into groups of five or six. Each group is given the task of building the highest possible "tower" out of the available materials in a fixed time period. The group must decide who will be responsible for the various activities required to build the tower. Materials might consist of the following, or variations or combinations thereof: small boxes (cereal boxes, for example), construction paper and Scotch tape, rolls from inside paper towels, pieces of styrofoam, metal scraps, etc. The only restriction is that the tower may not be attached in any way to the ceiling for support.

Problems in which students have to list all possible outcomes lend themselves well to the group discussion method. It is the group's decision as to when all outcomes have been listed.

PROBLEM   Orange drops are 3 for 10¢. Peppermints cost 5¢ each. Joan bought 20 pieces of candy. How many orange drops and how many peppermints did she buy?

While we do not advocate that students solve all problems in groups, the group process is a good method for allowing students to develop a respect for one another's abilities, and to learn to look for many possibilities in solving problems.

7. Encourage the use of freehand drawings.

Drawings do help students in problem solving. However, a beginning problem solver has a tendency to "measure" to find an answer, rather than to think the problem through or to demonstrate its solution mathematically. The use of freehand drawings will discourage students from relying on their drawings for measuring the answer. This does not mean, however, that you should allow or accept sloppy, inaccurate sketches. Students should draw neat, carefully labeled diagrams. Perpendiculars should look as if they form 90° angles; equal lengths should be drawn approximately equal.

This means, too, that the teacher must serve as a model for the students. When drawing diagrams at the board, make them carefully, but without the use of tools that differ from those the students may use. While rulers should not be used, a straightedge might be allowed. Practice in making freehand drawings is essential, since few teachers are so artistically inclined that they can draw well the first few times they attempt freehand drawings.

ACTIVITY   Draw various figures on several 3″ x 5″ cards. Spatial geometry offers many suitable drawings for this activity. Give one card to a student. Allow him or her to study the card for one minute. At the end of that time, the student must give back the card and try to replicate the drawing on the board. Then give the card back, or ask the rest of the class if they can decide what was drawn.

ACTIVITY   Prepare several transparencies of simple figures. Project these for thirty seconds to one minute, depending on the complexity of the drawing. When the projector is turned off, have each student attempt to reproduce the figure. Have each student compare his or her response with other students', and then with the original drawing.

ACTIVITY   Relate a simple situation to the class orally, and then have students prepare a sketch to illustrate the problem.

8. Suggest alternatives when the present approach has apparently yielded all possible information.

The mind-set (preconceived idea) that many students have often leads them to a dead end. This is not unusual, nor is it unexpected. This mind-set must be changed and another approach undertaken if the student has exhausted all possible information and has still not found a solution. It is at this point that some teachers err; they often direct the students through the most efficient path to the solution, rather than allowing further exploration to take place.

PROBLEM

In Figure 3–3, *AB* and *CD* are perpendicular diameters of length 8 centimeters, intersecting at *O*. Any point *F* is selected on arc *AC*. Perpendiculars *FG* and *FH* are drawn to *OA* and *OC*, respectively. Find the length of segment *GH*.

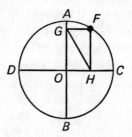

Figure 3–3

Discussion

In solving this problem, most students have a mind-set that suggests the use of the Pythagorean Theorem in triangle *GHO*. Once they have exhausted all the information in the problem, however, the teacher might suggest to them that they consider the rectangle *FGOH* and *both diagonals*.

PROBLEM

David is serving a fresh apple pie to his three brothers and himself. His older brother, Mike, bets his share that David cannot cut the pie into four equal portions without lifting his knife and/or going back over a cut. David thinks for a minute and then wins the bet. How does he do this?

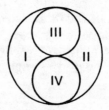

Figure 3–4

The Pedagogy of Problem Solving

Discussion   David cuts the pie with a "figure eight" cut passing through the center of the pie, as shown in Figure 3–4.

Since the radius of the original pie is r, its area equals πr^2. Thus the area of each small circle (labeled III and IV) is

$$\pi \cdot \left(\frac{r}{2}\right)^2 \qquad \text{or} \qquad \pi\frac{r^2}{4}$$

which is one-fourth of the original pie. By symmetry, portions I and II are equal. Thus each piece (I, II, III, IV) is one-fourth of the original pie. Once students rid themselves of the mind-set that the cuts must be straight lines, the problem can then be solved more readily.

PROBLEM   A pirate ship at point A in Figure 3–5 is 50 meters directly north of point C on the shore. Point D, also on the shore and due east of point C, is 130 meters from point C. Point B, a lighthouse, is due north of point D and 80 meters from point D. The pirate ship must touch the shoreline and then sail to the lighthouse. Find the location of point X on the shoreline so that the path from A to X to B will be a minimum.

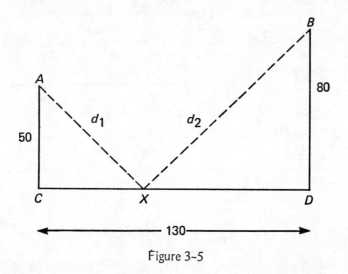

Figure 3–5

Discussion   If students decide to use a calculator, they can use a series of successive approximations, as follows:

CX	XD	d_1	d_2	$d_1 + d_2$	
0	130	50.0	152.6	202.6	
20	110	53.9	136.0	189.9	
40	90	64.0	120.4	184.44	
50	80	70.7	113.1	183.8 ←(approximate
60	70	78.1	106.3	184.41	location of
80	50	94.3	94.3	188.6	X)
100	30	104.4	85.4	189.8	
130	0	139.3	80.0	219.3	

Although these calculations do yield an approximate location for point X, the teacher might offer the following suggestions to students to help them "exactly" locate point X. The term "minimum distance" is the same as "shortest path." Students should realize that the shortest path between two points in a plane is a straight line. Thus, if we reflect segment BD its own length to B' so that B and B' are on opposite sides of CD, we can draw AB', as in Figure 3-6.

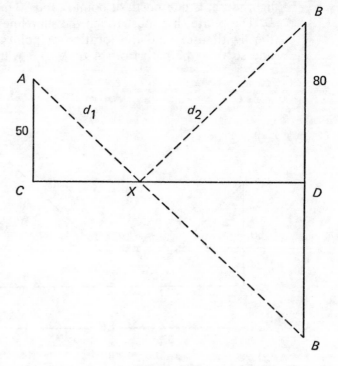

Figure 3-6

Now, since AB' is a minimum, and since triangle BDX is congruent to triangle $B'DX$, segment BX (or d_2) is equal to segment $B'X$. Thus point X is the exact location we wish.

When students are stuck, you might suggest that they look back at other problems they have solved in the past that were similar to the problem under consideration. This might lead to some ideas of what to do. Even a suggestion as to what might be done at a particular point is sometimes in order. Thus you could suggest to students that "it might be a good idea" if they

1. made a guess and checked it.
2. made a table.
3. drew a diagram.
4. used a calculator.
5. used a physical model.
6. worked backwards.
7. tried simpler numbers.

Even encouraging students to simply pause and carefully reflect on the problem is a good technique to try when students are totally stymied.

9. Raise creative, constructive questions.

Questions provide some student guidance, but at the same time allow students a wide range of responses. Give them time to think before they attempt to respond to your question. Research indicates that most teachers do not allow sufficient time for children to think about the question that is being asked them—the average teacher expects student response within three seconds. Problem solving is a complex process; it requires time for reflection. Don't rush your students.

Use open-ended questions as frequently as possible. Questions such as "How many . . . ?", "Count the number of . . . ", "Find all . . . ", "Prove that . . . " are non-threatening kinds of questions that lead to successful responses.

PROBLEM   How many triangles can you find in Figure 3-7?

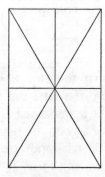

Figure 3-7

Discussion   The above question cannot be answered incorrectly, even if the student can find only a minimal number of triangles.

Throughout the problem-solving process, let your questions cause the students to reflect back on the problem solution. Too often we tend to turn away from a problem that has been "solved" (i.e., for which an answer has been found) in order to move on to the next problem. Thus we miss a chance to glean extra values from our energy. Examine the solution carefully; ask questions about key points. Ask many "What if . . . " questions. Ask students "What new question does this suggest?" or "How else might I ask this question?"

Other questions that you might ask include:

1. Do you recognize any patterns?
2. What is another way to approach the problem?
3. What kind of problem does this remind you of?
4. What would happen if . . .
    the conditions of the problem were changed to . . . ?
    the converse were asked?
    we imposed additional conditions?
5. What further exploration of this problem can you suggest?

10. Emphasize creativity of thought and imagination.

In a positive classroom atmosphere, students can be as free-thinking as they wish. You should not penalize "way out" answers if they show some thought on the part of the students. Again, keep in mind that it is the problem-solving *process* that is important!

ACTIVITY   A student's response to the question "How can I divide 25 pieces of candy among three people?" was "I'll take 23 pieces and give 1 to each of my friends!" Discuss the answer.

ACTIVITY   Karen drove from New York to Atlanta in 16 hours, a total distance of 800 miles. How fast did she drive? Discuss this problem.

Notice that the two activities suggested above yield answers that may be quite different from those expected. The student's interpretation of what is being asked is different, yet appropriate in thought. It leaves room for a good discussion.

Systematic trial and error and careful, selective guessing are both creative techniques to use. (How many times have teachers been heard to say to a student, "Do you *know*, or are you just guessing?") Guessing, or careful trial and error, should be practiced and encouraged. It is difficult but important to be a good guesser.

PROBLEM I am thinking of 2 two-digit numbers. They have the same digits, only reversed. The difference between the numbers is 54, while the sum of the digits of each number is 10. Find the 2 numbers.

Discussion While most algebra students could complete this problem by solving a pair of linear equations in two unknowns simultaneously, creative use of trial and error makes this problem suitable for a problem-solving activity at other levels as well. The teacher might suggest the following steps:

1. List all the two-digit numbers whose digit sum is 10:

$$19, 28, 37, 46, 55, 64, 73, 82, 91$$

2. Subtract pairs with the same digits:

$$91 - 19 = 72$$
$$82 - 28 = 54$$
$$73 - 37 = 36$$
$$64 - 46 = 18$$

At this point, you might consider asking the students how they know that 82, 28 is the *only* pair of two-digit numbers that satisfies the original problem.

PROBLEM Peggy and Barbara each want to buy a turkey for Thanksgiving. Peggy needs a larger turkey, since she has a bigger family. The butcher has two turkeys left. He tells the women that "Together they weigh a total of 20 pounds, and the smaller one costs 2¢ a pound more than the larger one.' Barbara pays $3.36 for the smaller one, while Peggy pays $5.98 for the larger. How much does each weigh?

Discussion Although the problem can be solved algebraically quite readily, let's see if we can solve the problem with systematic trial and error. Suppose we assume that the small turkey weighs, say, 8 pounds. Then the larger turkey must weigh 20 − 8 or 12 pounds. Since the bigger bird cost $5.98, the price per pound must have been 5.98/12, or almost 50¢. The smaller bird cost 2¢ per pound more, or 52¢, per pound. But only $3.36 was actually spent, and 8 × .52 ≠ 3.36.

Our next try should be a smaller weight for the smaller bird. In one or two more tries, we should arrive at the solution of 7 pounds and 13 pounds.

Puzzle problems that involve practice in arranging and rearranging numbers are helpful in developing student skills at organized guessing.

PROBLEM   Which disk in Figure 3–8 would you move to another box so that all three boxes would then have a sum of 15? Show your move.

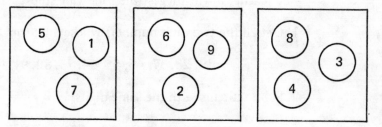

Figure 3–8

PROBLEM   Place the numbers 1, 2, 3, 4, 5, and 6 in the spaces provided in Figure 3–9 so that each side of the triangle adds up to 10.

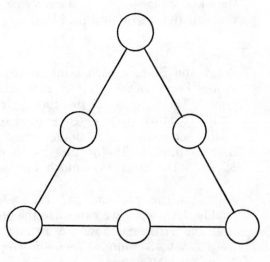

Figure 3–9

To help your students practice their guessing and estimating techniques, you might use several activities similar to the following.

ACTIVITY   Find a book with a lot of pages. Close your eyes and place a bookmark anywhere in the book. Now open your eyes and look at the bookmark. Guess the number of the page it is marking. Try this five times. Keep a record of how many times your guess was within 15 pages of the bookmark.

ACTIVITY   Close your eyes and guess how long a minute is. Check with a clock. See if you can come within 15 seconds, then within 10 seconds, then within 5 seconds. Record how close you come each time.

Activities such as these will help your students to improve their ability to estimate answers. Most of all, such practice will encourage them to "take a guesstimate." In itself, this is an important part of problem solving.

11. Encourage your students to use a calculator.

Over a hundred million hand-held minicalculators have been sold in the United States. The majority of your students probably either own a calculator or have access to one owned by someone within their immediate household. A teacher can provide conceptual experience long before the student makes the generalization, and concepts can often be extended to the real world through the use of the calculator. All students can add, subtract, multiply, and divide with a calculator. They can work with problems that are interesting and significant, even though the computations may be beyond their paper-and-pencil capacity. The focus can now be on problem solving for problem solving's sake; strategies and processes can be emphasized, with less time devoted to the computation within the problem-solving context.

PROBLEM   What is the largest whole number you can multiply by 6 and still have a product less than 79?

Discussion   Students can readily multiply each of the numbers in turn, beginning with 1×6, 2×6, etc., until they find a product that is more than 78.

PROBLEM   In the given array find the number that is missing. (*Note:* This is an array of numbers whose rows and columns should all add up to the same sum.)

211	121	181
145	?	205
157	229	127

PROBLEM   A gross of pencils is 144 pencils. If each pencil is 18 centimeters long, how long would the line be if all the pencils in a gross were put end to end?

Discussion   Students should decide whether their answer will be a number of pencils or a number of centimeters. Once they have decided what to do, the operation may be done easily with a calculator. Suppose the students form a regular 100-gon. What is its perimeter? (*Note:* This can be extended to an area problem.)

PROBLEM   Juanita likes to give her answers in large numbers. When asked her age, she replied that she has been alive a total of 7,358,400 minutes. How many years has Juanita been alive? (Consider a year as having 365 days.)

Discussion   The students will have to change the minutes to hours, the hours to days, and the days to years. What operation(s) will these calculations involve? Suppose Juanita decided to give her age in seconds. For how many seconds has she been alive?

PROBLEM   A major hamburger chain sold 22 billion hamburgers, each 1 inch thick. If we stacked these hamburgers, how many miles high would the stack be?

Discussion   Since the number 22 billion has 11 digits, it will not fit on most calculator displays. Hence students might multiply 5,280 by 12 to find out how many hamburgers there are in 1 mile. This number is then divided into 22 billion to get the answer 347,222.22 miles.

12. Use strategy games in class.

Games have a strong appeal for children and adults alike. In fact, most people enjoy games. Witness the many books of puzzles and games that are sold in bookstores, and the puzzle and game sections that appear on napkins in restaurants or in magazines on the airlines. Currently a new wave of strategy games utilizing a microprocessor is appearing.

    Children have been exposed to games and gaming all of their lives. They have learned what a game is, that games have rules to be followed, and that it is often possible to win a particular game consistently by developing a strategy to follow. Most of your students are already familiar with some of the basic strategy games, such as tic-tac-toe, checkers, and chess. They already know some basic strategies for these games.

To students, games are real-world problem situations. They want to win! And they enjoy playing games. Remember that skills which are acquired under enjoyable conditions are usually retained for longer periods of time than are skills acquired under stress or other adverse conditions.

When we develop a strategy for winning at a strategy game, we usually go through a series of steps that closely parallel those used in a heuristic system for solving problems.

Strategy Gaming

1. Read the game rules. Understand the play of the game. What is a "move"? What pieces are used? What does the board look like? What is a "win"? When is a game over?
2. Correlate the rules with those from any related game. Is there a similar game whose strategy you know? Select several possible lines of play to follow in an attempt to win the game.
3. Carry out your line of play. Can you counter your opponent's moves as the game proceeds?
4. Look back. If your strategy produced a win, will it work every time? Try alternative lines of play, alternative moves.

The similarity between this sequence and the one we suggested in Chapter 2 is marked indeed.

In order to use strategy games effectively with your students, you need a variety of games. These games can be found in many places. Best of all, games already known to the students can be varied by changing the rules, the pieces, or the game board. In these cases, students need not spend an inordinate amount of time learning all about a "new" game, but can immediately move on to developing a strategy for the play.

PROBLEM   Most of your students already know the game of tic-tac-toe. Under the usual rules, the player who first gets three of his or her own marks (usually X's and O's) in a straight line, either vertically, horizontally, or diagonally, is the winner. A simple rule change might be that the first player who gets three of his or her own marks in a straight line is the loser. This creates an entirely new line of play and requires a different strategy.

You can find many examples of strategy games in a local toy store or by looking through the many game and puzzle books available in bookstores. A brief collection of strategy games has been suggested in Section A.

13. Have your students flow-chart their own problem-solving process.

Students should realize that they are gradually developing their own set of heuristics, or problem-solving techniques. They should be made to recognize the components of their strategy. Therefore, after students have gone through the problem-solving process several times, ask them to list and then to flow-chart the steps they have used. At first, the flowchart might be a simple one, like the one in Figure 3-10.

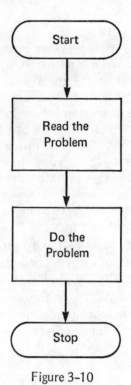

Figure 3-10

However, as the problem-solving process continues to develop, the flowchart should become more complex, like the one in Figure 3-11.

Notice that the students are now beginning to ask themselves questions. This is extremely important in the problem-solving process, as we have stated before.

After more and more experiences with the problem-solving process, a student might evolve a problem-solving flowchart like the one in Figure 3-12.

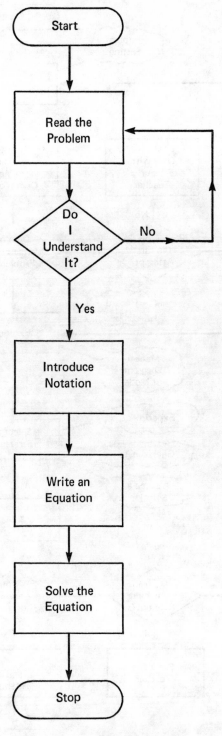

Figure 3-11

59

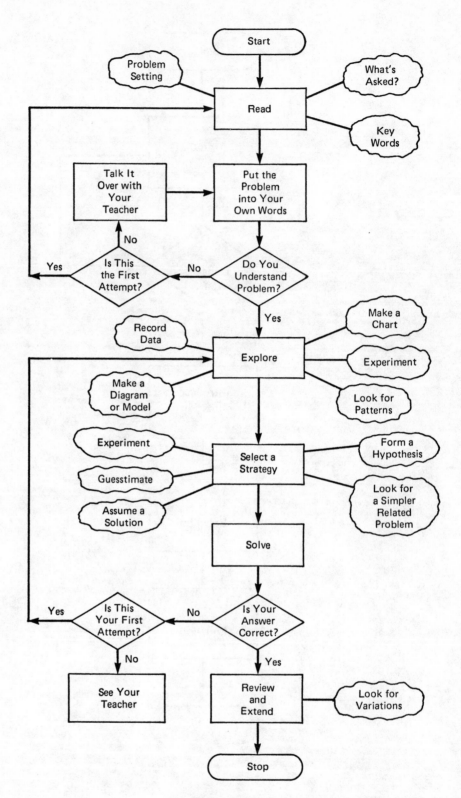

Figure 3-12

60

The preparation of a flowchart for problem solving is an extremely valuable procedure for both the students and the teacher. It will help the students to better organize their own thoughts. (We feel that anyone who cannot flow-chart a process does not really understand that process.) At the same time, it will provide the teacher with a chance to examine the problem-solving process as the students perceive it. It is a visual example of what the students are thinking as they solve a problem.

14. Don't teach new mathematics while teaching problem solving.

The developing of problem-solving skills, not the mathematics involved, is the paramount reason for discussing problems. The textbook exercises labeled "verbal problems" are exercises intended to develop some mathematical skill. Such a focus can easily mask the problem-solving aspect of the activity. Try to keep the mathematics involved in your problems well within the students' level of ability. In some cases, find problems where the math is a relatively minor part of the activity.

PROBLEM   Three boxes each contain a number of billiard balls. One box contains only even-numbered billiard balls, one box contains only odd-numbered billiard balls, and the third box contains a mixture of odd- and even-numbered billiard balls. *All* of the boxes are mislabeled. By selecting one ball from one of the boxes, can you correctly label the three boxes? Why or why not?

Discussion   One approach to the solution of this problem is to identify all the possible cases and try them. The other method is to recognize that, if you draw an even-numbered ball from the box labeled "odd," it might belong either to the box containing only even-numbered balls or to the box containing balls with both odd and even numbers. Because of the symmetry of the cases, selecting an odd-numbered ball from the box labeled "even" would create the same doubt. Thus, by selecting a ball from the box labeled "mixed" we can solve the problem. If the ball has an even number, the box must be relabeled "even," since the "mixed" label must be incorrect. Thus the box labeled "odd" must be relabeled "mixed," and the box labeled "even" must be relabeled "odd." Analogous reasoning is used to discuss the relabeling

61

process if an odd-numbered ball is selected from the box originally labeled "mixed."

PROBLEM   Sixteen teams are entered in a basketball elimination tournament. Winners play winners until only 1 team is left. What is the total number of games that must be played?

Discussion   This problem can be done by setting up an elimination diagram, as in Figure 3–13.

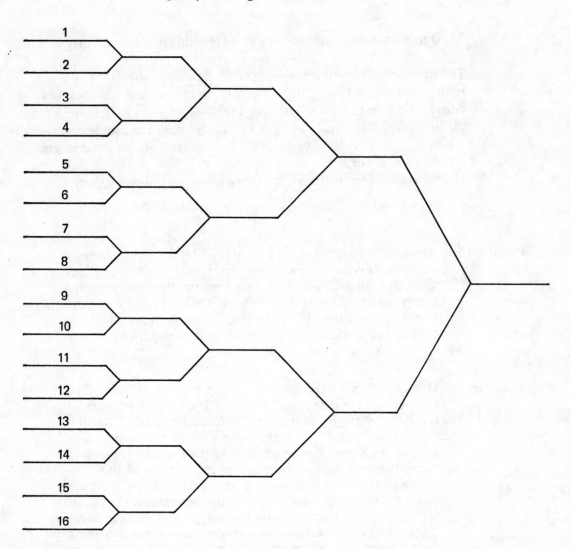

Number of games: 8 + 4 + 2 + 1 = 15

Figure 3-13

There is another more artistic solution to this problem, however. Since 1 team is eliminated in each game played and we must eliminate 15 teams, 15 games are needed to leave 1 team the final winner.

PROBLEM Three missionaries and three cannibals wish to cross a river. There is a boat that can carry up to three people, and either the missionaries or the cannibals can operate the boat. However, it is never permissible for the cannibals to outnumber the missionaries, either in the boat or on either shore. What is the smallest number of trips needed to make the crossing?

Discussion Although there is a great deal of problem solving involved in this problem, there is no computation. Students must realize that trips *back* across the river are the key to the problem. Thus the pattern that successfully solves the problem is

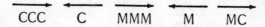

CCC   C   MMM   M   MC

or a total of 5 trips.

Although we have shown examples of problems that contain little mathematics to cloud the problem-solving issue, we want to point out that problems containing mathematics should also be used. If the mathematics level is kept within the abilities of the students, the problem-solving process will emerge as the primary goal of the activity.

PROBLEM A total of 642 digits were written in numbering the pages of a book. The writer was paid at the rate of 1¢ per digit. Thus he received 1¢ for writing a one-digit number, 2¢ for writing a two-digit number, and so on. How many pages did the book contain? If each page cost 5¢ to print, how much did it cost to print the entire book?

Discussion The writer wrote 9 one-digit numbers (1 through 9), and a total of 90 two-digit numbers (10 through 99). Thus he had written 189 digits when he reached page 99. This left 642 − 189 or 453 additional digits for the three-digit numbers (100 through 999). Dividing by 3, we find that he wrote 151 page numbers of three digits each. Thus the book contained a total of 151 + 90 + 9 or 250 pages.

Notice that the mathematics in this problem probably would not be too difficult for the average eighth or ninth grader to follow. Thus the problem-solving process could easily be emphasized, without being "cluttered up" by the mathematics.

A
Collection
of
Strategy
Games

TIC-TAC-TOE VARIATIONS

Since the basic game of tic-tac-toe is already known to most students, it becomes a logical place to find a wide assortment of variations.

1. Reverse Tic-Tac-Toe

This game has already been described in Chapter 3. It simply changes the requirements for a "win." Students must take turns placing an X or an O on the board, and try to *avoid* getting three marks in a row.

2. Triangular Tic-Tac-Toe

This game uses the basic rule—that is, the player scoring three of his or her marks in a straight line is the winner. The playing surface, however, has been changed into the triangular array shown in Figure A-1, rather than the usual square array.

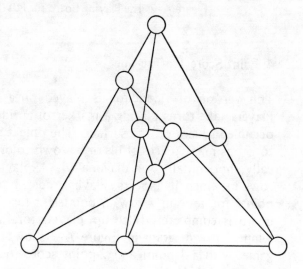

Figure A–1. The Playing Board for Triangular Tic-Tac-Toe

3. Put 'Em Down Tic-Tac-Toe

Instead of making marks on a tic-tac-toe board, each player is provided with three markers or other playing pieces. These are alternately placed on any of the line intersections (circles) on the playing surface in Figure A–2. The center circle may *not* be used by either player as his or her first play. After all the playing pieces have been placed, each player in turn moves one of his or her own pieces along a line to the next vacant cell. The winner is the first player to get three of his or her own pieces in a row, either vertically, horizontally, or diagonally.

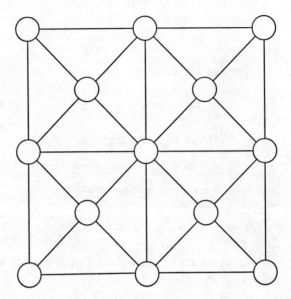

Figure A-2. The Playing Board for Put 'Em Down Tic-Tac-Toe

4. Point Score Tic-Tac-Toe

This version of tic-tac-toe is played on a 25-square playing surface. Players take turns placing a marker of an identifiable color in any un-occupied square on the surface. The object of the game is for a player to get as many pieces of his or her own color as possible in a row (verti-cally, horizontally, or diagonally). A playing piece is counted in all rows in which it appears. Players score 1 point for three in a row, 2 points for four in a row, 5 points for five in a row. When the square board is completely filled up, players total up their scores to find the winner. The diagram in Figure A-3 shows the playing surface for the game, with a 1-point and 2-point score (horizontally and diagonally, respectively). Notice how one marker counts twice, once in each row.

5. Wild Card Tic-Tac-Toe

This version of tic-tac-toe is played on the traditional 3 x 3 square array commonly used in tic-tac-toe. The variation in this version allows either player to put either mark anywhere on the playing surface when his or her turn comes. (Either an X or an O may be placed by either player at any time during the game.) The winner is the player who *completes* a straight line of three marks of either kind in his or her turn.

68

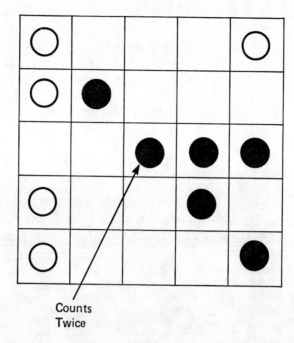

Counts
Twice

Figure A–3. The Playing Board for Point Score Tic-Tac-Toe

6. Three-Person Tic-Tac-Toe

Most versions of tic-tac-toe are games between two players. In this version, however, three people play. Players use either an X, an O, or an I as a marker, and the game is played on a board that contains 6 x 6 or 36 squares. Players put their own mark anywhere on the playing surface in turn. The first player to get three of his or her own marks in a row is the winner.

7. Big 7 Tic-Tac-Toe

This game is played on a playing surface consisting of 49 squares in a 7 x 7 array. Two players take turns placing either an X or an O anywhere on the playing surface. Each places his or her own mark. The first player to get four marks in a row is the winner.

8. Double Trouble Tic-Tac-Toe

This game is played on a 25-square (5 x 5) board. Players take turns placing either two X's or two O's anywhere on the board. The first player to get four of his or her marks in a row horizontally, vertically, or diagonally is the winner.

9. As You Wish Tic-Tac-Toe

This game is played on a 25-square (5 x 5) playing surface. Each player in turn may place on the board as many X's or O's as he or she wishes, provided they are all in the same vertical or horizontal row. The player who puts his or her mark into the twenty-fifth or last vacant cell on the board is the winner.

10. Dots-in-a-Row Tic-Tac-Toe

The game is played on a surface as shown in Figure A-4. Players take turns crossing out as many dots as they desire, provided the dots all lie in the same straight line. The player who crosses out the last dot is the winner.

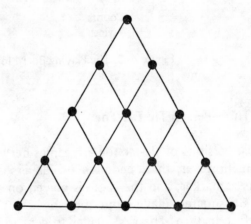

Figure A-4. The Dots-in-a-Row Board

11. Tac-Tic-Toe

This game is played on a 4 x 4 square surface. Each player has four chips or markers of a single color. The starting position is shown in Figure A-5. Players take turns moving a single piece of their own color. A move consists of moving one piece onto a vacant square either horizontally or vertically, but not diagonally. There is no jumping or capturing in this game. No piece can be moved into an already occupied square, but must be moved into an open, adjacent square. The player who moves three of his or her own pieces into a row, either horizontally, vertically, or diagonally, with no intervening spaces or intervening squares occupied by an opponent's piece, is the winner.

70

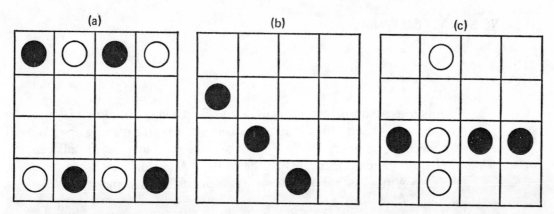

Figure A-5. (a) Starting Position for Tic-Tac-Toe. (b) A Win Position for Tic-Tac-Toe. (c) Nobody Wins in These Positions.

12. Tac-Tic-Toe, Chinese Version

This game is played on the surface shown in Figure A-6. Players use four chips, each player having a different color. Starting position is as shown in Figure A-6. Each player may move only his or her own chips. A move involves placing one of one's own pieces into an adjacent, vacant cell, following the lines on the board. There is no jumping and no capturing. The player who places three of his or her own pieces in the same straight line, with no vacant spaces intervening and none of the opponent's pieces intervening, is the winner.

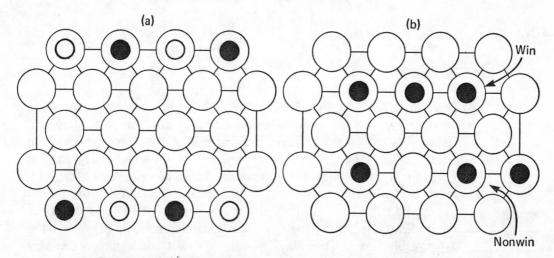

Figure A-6. (a) Starting Position for Tac-Tic-Toe, Chinese Version. (b) A Winning Position and a Nonwinning Position.

BLOCKING STRATEGY GAMES

13. Blockade

Playing pieces are placed on cells A and B in Figure A-7 for player 1, and on cells C and D for player 2. Players take turns moving one playing piece along lines on the playing surface into any vacant, adjacent circle. No jumps or captures are permitted. A player loses when he or she cannot move either of his or her two pieces in his or her turn.

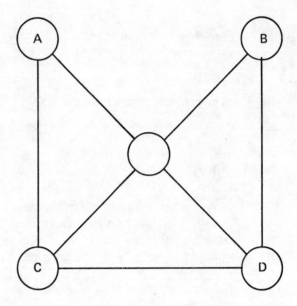

Figure A-7. Playing Surface for Blockade

14. Pawns

This game is played on a 3 x 3 array of squares. Each player has three chips or markers of a single color. Starting position is as shown in Figure A-8. Players take turns moving one of their own pieces. Each piece may be moved one square forward, or one square diagonally if a capture is made. A diagonal move can be made *only* with a capture, and a capture cannot be made on a forward move. A captured piece is removed from the board. A player is a winner when he or she either (1) places one piece in the opponent's starting row, or (2) makes the last possible move on the playing board. As a variation, players can play the game on a 4 x 4 or a 5 x 5 board, with an adjusted number of pieces.

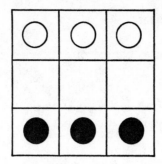

Figure A-8. Starting Position for Pawns

15. Hex

The game of Hex is played on a diamond-shaped board made up of hexagons. (See Figure A-9.) The players take turns placing an X or an O in any hexagon on the board. The winner is the first player to make an unbroken path from one side of the board to the other. Blocking moves and other strategies should be developed as the game proceeds. The corner hexagons can belong to either player.

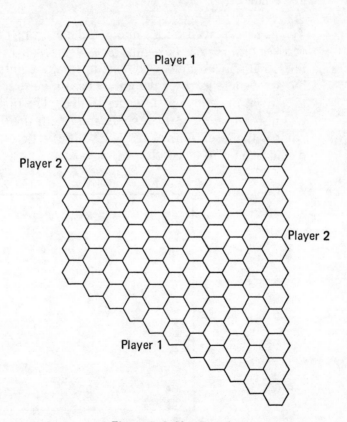

Figure A-9. Hex Board

16. Bi-Squares

The game is played on a playing surface that consists of 16 squares in one long continuous row. Players take turns placing their mark (an X for player 1 and an O for player 2) into each of two adjacent, unoccupied squares on the board. The player who makes the last successful move on the board is the winner.

17. Domino Cover

This game is played on a standard 8 x 8 checkerboard, and uses a set of dominoes that will cover two adjacent squares, either horizontally or vertically. Players take turns placing a domino anywhere on the board, according to the following rules: (1) player 1 can only place dominoes in a horizontal direction; (2) player 2 can only place dominoes in a vertical direction. The loser is the player who cannot make a move by placing a domino in the correct position.

18. Triahex

The game is played on a game board consisting of 6 points that are the vertices of a regular hexagon. (See Figure A–10.) There are exactly 15 lines that can be drawn connecting the 6 points. The game is played by two people, each of whom uses a different colored marker. Players take turns drawing any 1 of the 15 lines. The first player who is forced to finish a triangle formed *completely* with the lines of his or her own color is the loser. Only a triangle whose vertices are points of the original hexagon is to be considered.

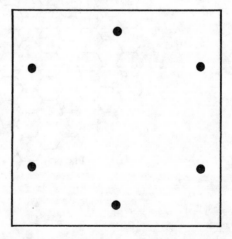

Figure A–10. The Six Vertices of a Regular Hexagon in Triahex

19. Dodge 'Em

The game is played on a 3 x 3 square board with two black checkers and two white ones. Starting position is shown in Figure A-11. Black sits on the south side of the board, white on the west side. Players may move a checker forward or to their left or right, unless the checker is blocked by another counter of either color or the edge of the playing surface. Each player's goal is to move all of his or her pieces off the far side of the board. Black moves north, west, or east, and tries to move all of his or her pieces off the board on the north side; white moves east, north, or south, and tries to move his or her pieces off the board on the east side. There are no captures or jumps. A player must always leave the opponent a legal move or forfeit the game. The first player to get his or her two pieces off the board is the winner.

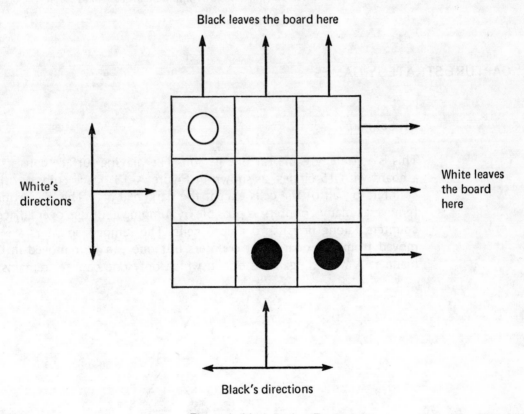

Figure A-11. A Dodge 'Em Board

20. Tromino Saturation

The game is played on a 5 x 5 square board. The playing pieces consist of the two basic tromino shapes shown in Figure A-12. Each tromino piece should exactly cover three squares on the playing surface. Players take turns placing one of the pieces of either shape anywhere on the playing surface. The first player who cannot place a piece to exactly cover three squares is the loser. (In order to allow each player a full choice of which piece to select on each play, prepare eight pieces of each kind.) If the size of the board is increased to a 6 x 6 square board, prepare twelve of each piece.

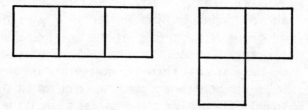

Figure A-12. The Two Basic Tromino Shapes for Saturation

CAPTURE STRATEGY GAMES

21. Solitaire

This is a strategy game for one person. The playing surface consists of a board with 15 circles, as shown in Figure A-13. Place chips or other counters on all of the cells except the darkened cell. The player must remove as many counters as possible by jumping counters over adjacent counters (along lines) into empty cells. The jumped counters are removed from the board. All counters but one can be removed in this manner. A winning game is one in which only one counter remains. A

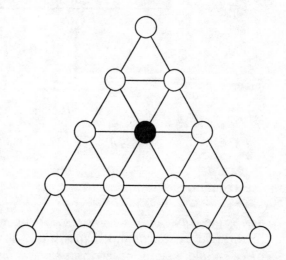

Figure A-13. A Solitaire Board

76

variation for experienced players is to try to make the one remaining counter end the game in the darkened cell.

22. Spot

Spot is played on a circular playing surface, as shown in Figure A-14. Place a penny on spot 2, a dime on spot 15. Players take turns; one moves the penny, the other moves the dime. Moves are made along any solid line into an adjacent spot. The penny moves first. The object of the game is for the penny to "capture" the dime by moving into the spot the dime occupies. The capture must be made within six moves. The penny player loses if he or she has failed to catch the dime by the end of his or her sixth move.

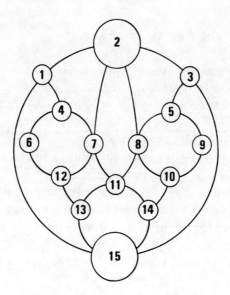

Figure A-14. A Spot Playing Surface

23. Fox and Geese

This game, for two players, is played on a surface with 33 cells, as shown in Figure A-15. The fox marker and the thirteen goose markers are placed as shown. The fox can move in any direction along a line—up, down, left, or right. The geese may not move backwards. The fox can capture a goose by making a short jump over a single goose along a line into the next cell, provided that cell is vacant. The fox can make successive jumps on any one turn, provided vacant cells exist. The geese win if they can corner the fox so that he cannot move. The fox wins if he captures enough geese so that they cannot corner him.

77

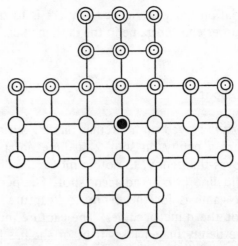

Figure A-15. Starting Position for Fox and Geese

24. The Wolf and the Farmers

One player has a single playing piece, the wolf. The other player has seven farmers. The wolf begins by placing his piece on the top circle of the triangular board in Figure A-16. The second player places one farmer anywhere else on the board. Each time the wolf moves, an additional farmer is placed on the board. All pieces move the same way, one circle at a time, along the marked lines. However, the farmers may not move until all of them have been entered on the board. The farmers may not capture; the wolf captures by jumping over a farmer along a line to a next cell, which must be vacant. The jumped piece is removed from the board. Successive captures are allowed. The wolf wins if he captures enough farmers so that they cannot confine him. The farmers win if they succeed in confining the wolf so that he cannot move.

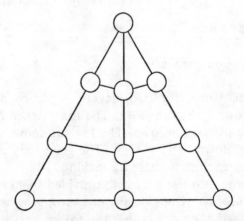

Figure A-16. Playing Surface for the Wolf and the Farmers

25. Sprouts

Three dots are placed in a triangular array on a piece of paper. Players take turns drawing a line connecting any two dots, or connecting a dot to itself. After a line is drawn, a new dot is placed approximately midway between the two dots being connected, along the connecting line. No lines may cross, and no more than three lines may terminate in a single point. The last player to make a successful move is the winner. See Figure A–17. The new point *D* is shown along the line connecting point *A* to itself. The new point *E* is shown along the line connecting *B* to *C*. Notice that points *D*, *A*, and *E* each have two lines terminating.

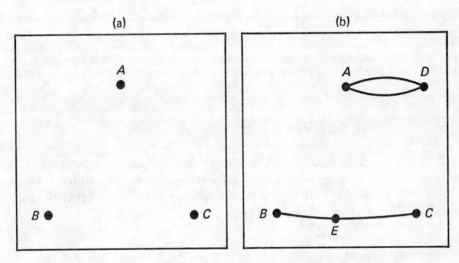

Figure A–17. (a) A Sprouts Board. (b) Typical Moves in Sprouts

26. Square-Off

The game is played on a checkerboard. Two players take turns placing one checker anywhere on the board. Each player uses checkers of one color. The game continues until the checkers of one color form the vertices of a square of any size. The player using that color is declared the winner.

SOME COMMERCIAL STRATEGY GAMES

27. Basis

A strategy game in which players form numerals in different bases, while preventing their opponents from doing the same. (Holt, Rinehart and Winston Company)

28. Battleship

A game of strategy in which two players try to sink each other's ships, which are hidden from view. A good introduction to coordinates. (Creative Publications)

29. Bee Line

Players use strategy while attempting to make a "beeline" across the playing board. (SEE Corporation)

30. Block 'N Score

A strategy game in which two players work with binary notation. (Creative Publications)

31. Equations

A game designed to give students practice in abstract reasoning, to increase speed and accuracy in computing, and to teach some of the basic concepts of mathematics. The game can be varied to work in different bases. (Wff 'N Proof)

32. Foo (Fundamental Order of Operations)

A strategy game in which players try to combine seven cards into any multiple of 12. Extra cards are drawn and discarded until one player calls "Foo!" (Cuisenaire, Inc.)

33. Helix

Another three-dimensional tic-tac-toe game. Players place different colored beads on a series of pins, trying to get four in a row. The pins are not only in straight lines, but also along arcs designated on the playing surface. (Creative Publications)

34. Kalah

A strategy game involving counting, skill, and logic. Chance is a minimal factor. (Creative Publications)

35. Mastermind

A secret code of colored pegs is set up out of sight of one player. He or she then has ten chances to duplicate the colors and exact positions of the code pegs. Pure logic! (Cadaco, Invicta, Creative Publications)

36. Numble

A game similar to a crossword puzzle. Players place tiles with numerals from 0 to 9 on them to form addition, subtraction, multiplication, and division problems. (Math Media, Inc.)

37. On Sets

A series of games that teach some of the basic ideas of set theory and set language. Comes with an excellent manual. Involves union, intersection, complement, etc. (Wff 'N Proof)

38. Pressups

A player must guide the direction of play so as to press down pegs of his or her own color. Traps may be set. The winner is the player with more of his or her own pegs depressed. (Invicta)

39. Qubic

Qubic expands tic-tac-toe into a four-level space game. Players win by setting four markers in a straight line in one or several planes. (Parker Brothers)

40. Racko

By drawing from the pile players attempt to replace cards in their racks so that the numbers read from high to low in numerical sequence. (Milton Bradley Company)

41. Score Four

Similar to Qubic and Helix. Players place wooden beads on metal pins and need four in a row to score. (Lakeside Toys)

42. Soma Cube

An elegant cube with irregular sets of combinations of cubes. There are 1,105,920 mathematically different ways to come up with the 240 ways the seven SOMA pieces fit together to form the original cube. (Parker Brothers)

43. Tromino

Triangular wooden pieces extend the skills and principles needed for dominoes. A great deal of strategy is used as well as mathematical knowledge. (Creative Publications)

44. Tuf

A game designed to help students utilize the basic operations of mathematics. Students form equations using tiles with various numerals and operations on them. Both speed and accuracy count. (Avalon Hill Company)

45. Twixt

A board strategy game with moves and countermoves. Players try to connect a chain of linked pegs before their opponents can do the same (3-M Company)

46. Vectors

A game in which thought and ability are used to deceive opponents. The game utilizes a chess-like board with a single piece and cards. (Cuisenaire, Inc.)

47. Wff 'N Proof

The game is based on symbolic logic. Symbols are used to form logical sequences. (Wff 'N Proof)

A
Collection
of
Non-Routine
Problems

Problems 1–19 are particularly applicable to the elementary school student. Problems 20–31 are particularly applicable to the junior high school student. Problems 32–55 are particularly applicable to the senior high school student. Problems marked with an asterisk are easily adaptable to other levels.

PROBLEM 1   How many different ways can you make change for a 50¢ piece without using pennies?

Discussion   In order to organize the work, prepare a table.

Nickels (5¢)	Dimes (10¢)	Quarters (25¢)
10	0	0
9	–	– (cannot be done)
8	1	0
7	–	– (cannot be done)
6	2	0
5	0	1
4	3	0
3	1	1
2	4	0
1	2	1
0	5	0
0	0	2

Thus there are a total of 10 ways to satisfy the given conditions.

PROBLEM 2   One day a man entered a shop; he paid 1¢ to get in, spent one-half of the money he had, and then paid 1¢ to leave. He then paid 1¢ to enter a second shop, where he spent one-half of the money he had left and again paid 1¢ to leave. He then entered a third shop, where he again paid 1¢ to get in, spent one-half of the money he had left, and paid 1¢ to leave. Finally he entered a fourth shop, where he paid 1¢ to get in, spent one-half of the money he had left, and paid 1¢ to leave. On leaving the fourth shop, he found himself completely broke. How much money had he begun with?

Discussion   The problem lends itself to working backwards:

Shop 4   1¢   to leave
                 2¢   spent one-half
                 3¢   to enter

Shop 3   4¢   to leave
8¢   spent one-half
9¢   to enter

Shop 2   10¢   to leave
20¢   spent one-half
21¢   to enter

Shop 1   22¢   to leave
44¢   spent one-half
45¢   to enter

He began with 45¢.

*PROBLEM 3   Given the digits 1, 1, 2, 2, 3, 3, 4, 4, write an eight-digit number using these eight digits such that the

1's are separated by 1 digit;

2's are separated by 2 digits;

3's are separated by 3 digits;

4's are separated by 4 digits.

Discussion   Organized trial and error should yield several solutions similar to 2 3 4 2 1 3 1 4.

PROBLEM 4   A grocer has three pails: an empty pail that holds 5 liters, an empty pail that holds 3 liters, and an 8-liter pail that is filled with apple cider. Show how the grocer can measure exactly 4 liters of apple cider with the help of the 5-liter and 3-liter pails.

Discussion   Make a chart to show how the grocer might do the division.

3-liter pail	5-liter pail	8-liter pail
0	0	8
0	5	3
3	2	3
3	0	5
0	3	5
3	3	2
1	5	2
1	0	7
0	1	7
3	1	4

While this does yield an answer to the problem, notice that this answer is not a minimum number of pourings (not called for in the original problem). For example, the first three steps can be ignored; one could begin directly with step 4 (3 liters in the 3-liter pail, 5 liters left in the 8-liter pail). Students should be encouraged to go on to find the minimum number of pourings needed.

PROBLEM 5

In how many different ways can three people divide 25 pieces of candy so that each person gets at least 1 piece?

Discussion

We have

    3 pieces of candy: 1-1-1
    4 pieces of candy: 1-1-2; 1-2-1; 2-1-1
    5 pieces of candy: 1-1-3; 1-3-1; 3-1-1; 2-2-1; 2-1-2; 1-2-2

Prepare a chart.

Number of pieces of candy	3	4	5	6	7	...	n
Number of ways to distribute	1	3	6	10	15		$\dfrac{(n-1)(n-2)}{2}$

Thus, for 25 pieces of candy,

$$\frac{(24)(23)}{2} = 12 \times 23$$

$$= 276$$

There are 276 ways to distribute the pieces of candy.

PROBLEM 6

The new game in town is an addition game known as Eighteen. Players take turns placing a chip or marker on one of the numbers from 2 through 10. The first player to cover any three numbers whose sum is 18 is the winner. Jeff understands the game and has figured out a method so that he can never lose. (He may have a game end in a tie, however.) How does Jeff do this?

Discussion   Although the numbers in the Eighteen game are arranged in a row, Jeff, in his head, has placed the numbers in a typical magic square arrangement, as shown.

7	2	9
8	6	4
3	10	5

As the game is played, Jeff views it as a tic-tac-toe board. He plays either to win or to block. If he can play tic-tac-toe to win, then he can easily win at Eighteen.

PROBLEM 7   Nancy had 69¢ in coins. Jill asked her for change for a half-dollar. Nancy tried to make change, but found that she didn't have the correct coins to do so. What coins did she have, if each coin was less than a half-dollar?

Discussion   Trial and error will enable students to find that the coins were 1 quarter, 4 dimes, and 4 pennies.

PROBLEM 8   Given the sequence of numbers

$$2, 3, 5, 8$$

explain why the next number might be 12, or 13, or 2.

Discussion   There are a variety of ways in which the four given terms might have been arrived at. For example, if we regard these as members of a Fibonacci sequence, each term was arrived at by adding the preceding two terms. Thus, $2 + 3 = 5$, $3 + 5 = 8$, $5 + 8 = 13$, and so on. On the other hand, we might view the sequence as having been generated by adding increasing differences. Thus $2 + 1 = 3$, $3 + 2 = 5$, $5 + 3 = 8$, $8 + 4 = 12$, and so on. Then, too, this might be viewed as a cyclical series in which the four terms repeat. Thus the next term would be 2.

PROBLEM 9   What is the greatest number of coins you can use to make 35¢? What is the smallest number of coins you can use? In how many different ways can you make 35¢?

Discussion   The greatest number of coins is obviously 35 pennies. The smallest number of coins is 2 (1 dime, 1 quarter). To find the number of different ways change can be made, we can make a table.

Pennies	Nickels	Dimes	Quarters
35	—	—	—
30	1	—	—
25	—	1	—
25	2	—	—
•	•	•	•
•	•	•	•
•	•	•	•
—	—	1	1

PROBLEM 10

A woman has some cows and some chickens. Together the animals have a total of 54 legs. How many cows and how many chickens might she have?

Discussion

We have the restriction that cows have 4 legs and chickens have only 2 legs. Since 54 is not evenly divisible by 4, she must have at least 1 chicken. We now form a table to organize our results:

Cows	Legs	Chickens	Legs	Total number of legs
13	52	1	2	54
12	48	2	4	54
11	44	5	10	54
etc.				

We might extend the question by asking if it is possible to have exactly 3 chickens, 4 chickens, etc., and why.

PROBLEM 11

How many different combinations of 2 Cuisenaire rods can be placed end to end to form a length equal to an orange rod?

PROBLEM 12

Two students in the local elementary school have a business selling apples. Each has 30 apples to sell. Allen wants to sell his apples at 5¢ each, while Suzy wants to sell her apples at 3 for 10¢. They decide to merge their operations and to sell all 60 apples at 5 for 20¢. Which way would they make more money, and how much more would they make?

Discussion

Allen would sell his 30 apples at 5¢ each, receiving a total of 30 × .05 or $1.50. Suzy would sell her 30 apples at 3 for 10¢, receiving a total of $1.00. Together they would receive a total of $2.50. If they sell all 60 apples at 5 for 20¢, they will receive a total of $2.40. Thus they would make a profit of 10¢ more by selling the apples in the original manner.

PROBLEM 13

A typical jet plane uses a gallon of gasoline for every 5 miles it flies. If the Dogpatch Airliner travels at 375 miles an hour and has flown for 700 hours, how much gasoline has the airliner used? At 64¢ per gallon, how much has this gasoline cost the airline?

Discussion

If we multiply the miles per hour (375) by the number of hours flown (700), we obtain 262,500 miles flown. Dividing this by the number of miles per gallon (5), we obtain a total of 52,500 gallons of gasoline. Now we multiply this by 64¢ to find the total cost: $33,600. (Notice that this is an excellent problem to do with a calculator.)

PROBLEM 14

From Figure B-1 select 2 strips of paper whose lengths have a sum of 15 centimeters and a difference of 3 centimeters.

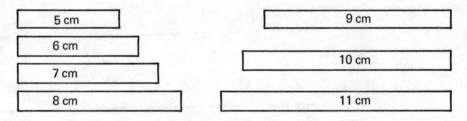

Figure B-1

Discussion

Students may begin by examining pairs of paper strips, the sum of whose lengths is 15 centimeters (10, 5; 9, 6; 8, 7), and then check for a difference of 3 centimeters. Others may decide to list all pairs of numbers together with their sums and differences.

*PROBLEM 15

Two girls wish to find the speed of a moving freight train as it passes by their town. They find that 42 railroad cars pass by the corner in 1 minute. The average length of a railroad car is 60 feet. At what speed is the train moving in miles per hour?

Discussion   If 42 railroad cars pass by the corner in 1 minute, then 60 × 42 or 2,520 cars pass by in 1 hour. This is a total length of 2,520 × 60 or 151,200 feet per hour. Dividing this by 5,280, we obtain 28.6363... miles per hour as the speed of the train. (Again, use of the calculator enables the problem-solving aspect to be emphasized.)

PROBLEM 16   What is the smallest number of pennies that can be arranged into 6 equal piles and also into 8 equal piles?

Discussion   Some students will multiply 6 × 8 and give 48 as their answer. This would be a correct solution if it were not for the requirement that the answer be the *smallest* number. Thus 24 is the correct answer. Notice that this problem can be done using chips, marbles, or bottlecaps.

PROBLEM 17   Stanley makes extra money by buying and selling comic books. He buys them for 7¢ each and sells them for 10¢ each. Stanley needs 54¢ to buy some batteries for his calculator. How many comic books must Stanley buy and sell to earn the 54¢?

Discussion   Some students will realize that Stanley earns 3¢ profit on each comic book. Thus they can divide 54¢ by 3¢ to find the number of comic books he must sell (18). Others will want to make a table:

Number of comics	1	2	3	4	5	6	7	...
Profit	3¢	6¢	9¢	12¢	15¢	18¢	21¢	...

PROBLEM 18   Luisa was playing darts. She threw 6 darts, and all 6 hit the target in Figure B–2. Which of the following could be her score?

4, 17, 56, 28, 29, 31

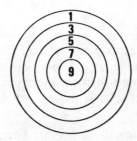

Figure B-2

91

Discussion   Since all 6 darts hit the target, Luisa's highest score could be 6 × 9 or 54; her lowest score could be 6 × 1 or 6. Furthermore, since there are only odd numbers on the target, the 6 hits must have an even sum. Thus only 28 is a possible score for Luisa. This score can be reached in a variety of ways:

$$9 + 9 + 5 + 3 + 1 + 1 = 28$$
$$9 + 7 + 7 + 3 + 1 + 1 = 28$$

etc.

*PROBLEM 19   A customer ordered 15 cupcakes. Cupcakes are placed in packages of 4, 3, or 1. In how many different ways can you fill the order?

Discussion   Students can arrange 15 chips or bottlecaps in groups of 4, 3, and 1 to total 15. This can be done in 15 ways:

4's	3's	1's
3	1	0
3	0	3
2	2	1
2	1	4
2	0	7
1	3	2
1	2	5
1	1	8
1	0	11
0	5	0
0	4	3
0	3	6
0	2	9
0	1	12
0	0	15

*PROBLEM 20   I am a proper fraction. The sum of my numerator and my denominator is 1 less than a perfect square. Their difference is 1 more than a perfect square. Their product is 1 less than a perfect square. What fraction am I?

Discussion   Examine those products that are 1 less than a perfect square.

Perfect square minus 1	Possible product	Sum	Difference
0	—	—	—
3	1 X 3	4	2
8	1 X 8	9	7
8	2 X 4	6	2
15	1 X 15	16	14
15	3 X 5	8	2

Thus one answer to the problem is the fraction 3/5.

PROBLEM 21   An old man on his way to market was knocked down. All the eggs he was going to sell were broken. When asked how many eggs he had had, the man replied, "I don't remember the exact number, but when they were put into piles of 2, there was 1 left over; in piles of 3, there was 1 left over. The same was true if I put them into piles of 4, piles of 5, and piles of 6. There was always 1 left over. However, if I put them into piles of 7, there were none left over." How many eggs did the old man have when he started?

Discussion   We multiply 2 X 3 X 4 X 5 X 6 and obtain 720. Adding the 1 left over, we obtain 721, which is exactly divisible by 7. Thus one possible answer is 721 eggs. However, is this the smallest number? Students might wish to examine all of the multiples of 7 until they can find one that leaves a remainder of 1 when divided by 2, by 3, by 4, by 5, and by 6. The first number that works is 301. Other answers might be revealed in a similar manner.

PROBLEM 22   Which of the following represents the cube of 156?

(a) 3,796,416   (c) 3,944,312
(b) 4,251,528   (d) 3,581,577

Discussion   Many students will simply cube 156 to find the answer. However, they should be encouraged to investigate the pattern that evolves when we cube numbers that have a final digit of 1, 2, 3, 4, etc. Only 6^3 will have a final digit of 6.

*PROBLEM 23   A cube that is 3 inches on each edge is painted completely red on all 6 faces. The cube is then cut into 27 smaller cubes, each measuring 1 inch on each edge. Of these 27 smaller cubes, how many have exactly 3 faces painted red? How many have exactly 2 faces painted red? How many have

93

exactly 1 face painted red? How many have no faces painted red?

Discussion
Examine the diagram in Figure B–3. We can see that each of the 8 corner pieces will have exactly 3 faces painted red; the center piece on each face will have exactly 1 painted surface (there are 6 of these); the single cube in the exact center of the original cube will have no painted faces. There will be exactly 12 small cubes having paint on exactly 2 faces (numbered 1, 2, 3, . . . in the diagram).

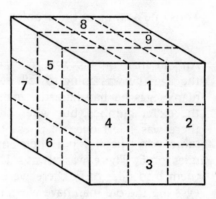

Figure B–3

PROBLEM 24
Two men were discussing the gasoline shortage and how to combat it. One told the other, "You know, Fred, I installed a new carburetor, and it saved me 36%. I then installed a new distributor, and it saved me 42%. I put on a set of new radial tires, and they saved me 53%. The mechanic tuned up the car and saved me 66%." Fred asked, "Now what happens?" "Well," said the first man, "whenever I drive anywhere, the car overflows!" What is your reaction to this story?

Discussion
We have

Percentage of gasoline used before "improvements"	100
Percentage of gasoline used with new carburetor	$100 - 36 = 64$
Percentage of gasoline used with new distributor	$64 - .42(64) = 37.12$
Percentage of gasoline used with new tires	$37.12 - .53(37.12) = 17.45$
Percentage of gasoline used after tuneup	$17.45 - .66(17.45) = 5.93 \approx 6$

Thus, a trip that used to require 100 gallons of gasoline before any improvements were made would now take about 6 gallons of gasoline, a rather "tall" story.

PROBLEM 25   A golfer had just finished a round of golf when someone asked her how she had done that day. She answered that her score was an unusual one in that, had she needed 20 more strokes, the result would have been a perfect square; had she needed 20 fewer strokes, that too would have been a perfect square. What was her actual score that day?

Discussion   We are looking for a number that need not be a perfect square itself. However, it must be 20 more than a perfect square and 20 less than a perfect square. By careful trial and error, we find that the answer is 101. ($101 - 20 = 81$; $101 + 20 = 121$.)

PROBLEM 26   Jeff and Mike bred tropical fish. Mike decided to abandon the hobby and give his fish away. First he gave half of them and half a fish more to Scott. Then he gave half of what was left and half a fish more to Billy. That left Mike with only 1 fish, which he gave to Jeff. How many fish did Mike start with?

Discussion   Although we can solve this problem algebraically, the equation formed is rather complicated:

$$x - \left(\frac{x}{2} + \frac{1}{2}\right) - \left[\frac{x - \left(\frac{x}{2} + \frac{1}{2}\right)}{2} + \frac{1}{2}\right] = 1$$

If we work backwards (and assume that Mike doesn't cut any fish in half), we realize that we are working with a set of odd numbers. Since only 1 fish remained after Mike's last gift, he must have had 3 fish before giving the 1 to Jeff (half of 3, or $1\frac{1}{2}$, plus $\frac{1}{2}$ equals 2). So his gift to Billy was 2 fish. Working backwards in a similar manner, we find that Mike must have started with 7 fish and given $3\frac{1}{2} + \frac{1}{2}$ (or 4) to Scott.

*PROBLEM 27   When I arrange the members of a marching band in rows of 2, 3, or 4, there is always 1 person left over. However, when I arrange them in rows of 5, the rows are all even. What is the minimum number of people in the marching band?

Discussion   The number has the property that it always leaves a remainder of 1 when divided by 2, 3, or 4. The smallest number

95

with this property is the LCM of 2, 3, and 4 with 1 added. The LCM of these numbers is 12; adding 1 we get 13. Thus the sequence that satisfies the requirements of the problem is 13, 25, 37, 49, 61, 73, 85, ... We know that the number is evenly divisible by 5, so the only possible answers at this point are 25 and 85. The minimum number is 25.

PROBLEM 28   If a brick balances with three-quarters of a brick plus three-quarters of a pound, then how much does the brick weigh?

Discussion   The three-quarters-of-a-pound weight must exactly balance the missing one-fourth of a brick. Thus 1/4 of a brick = 3/4 of a pound, and 4/4 of a brick = 4 times 3/4 of a pound, or 3 pounds.

PROBLEM 29   A textbook is opened at random. To what pages is it opened if the product of the facing page numbers is 3,192?

Discussion   Students can try pairs of successive numbers on their calculators until they find the product 3,192. An alternative method is to take the square root of 3,192. This gives 56.497787. Students then try the integers surrounding this number, namely 56 and 57.

PROBLEM 30   A pail with 40 washers in it weighs 175 grams. The same pail with 20 washers in it weighs 95 grams. How much does the pail weigh alone? How much does each washer weigh?

Discussion   Students can actually guess until they arrive at the answer (washers weigh 4 grams; the pail weighs 15 grams). Other students might reason in the following manner:

$$
\begin{array}{rl}
1 \text{ pail} + 20 \text{ washers} = & 95 \text{ grams} \\
\text{then } 2 \text{ pails} + 40 \text{ washers} = & 190 \text{ grams} \\
\text{but } \underline{1 \text{ pail} + 40 \text{ washers} = 175 \text{ grams}} \\
1 \text{ pail} \qquad\qquad = & 15 \text{ grams}
\end{array}
$$

$$
\begin{array}{rl}
1 \text{ pail} + 40 \text{ washers} = & 175 \text{ grams} \\
\underline{1 \text{ pail} + 20 \text{ washers} = \ \ 95 \text{ grams}} \\
20 \text{ washers} = & 80 \text{ grams} \\
1 \text{ washer} = & 4 \text{ grams}
\end{array}
$$

PROBLEM 31   The following advertisement appeared in the real estate section of a local newspaper:

If you were to buy an acre of land as advertised, what amount would you be required to pay?

Discussion In addition to teaching "number explosions," this problem introduces the topic of advertising and come-on programs. Mathematically it is an interesting problem for use with the calculator. The only information required is that an acre is 200' x 200'. Thus

$$(200 \times 12)(200 \times 12)(.05) = \$288,000 \text{ an acre}$$

PROBLEM 32 The probability of rolling a 2 on a standard pair of dice is 1/36; the probability of rolling a 3 is 2/36 (a 1-2 or a 2-1); and so on. How could you re-mark a pair of dice so that the probability of throwing each number from 1 through 12 was the same?

Discussion If the probability of throwing each number from 1 through 12 is to be the same, then each must have a probability of 3/36. To allow you to roll a 1, the pair of dice would have to be marked with a 1 and a 0. To obtain the required probability of 3/36, there must be 3 such situations. Thus the results should be

Die 1	Die 2
0, 1, 2	1, 1, 1
3, 4, 5	7, 7, 7

*PROBLEM 33 During the recent census, a man told the census-taker that he had three children. When asked their ages, he replied, "The product of their ages is 72. The sum of their ages is the same as my house number." The census-taker ran to the door and looked at the house number. "I still can't tell," she complained. The man replied, "Oh, that's right. I forgot to tell you that the oldest one likes chocolate pudding." The census-

97

taker promptly wrote down the ages of the three children. How old are they?

Discussion

List all the combinations of three numbers whose product is 72, together with their sums:

1-1-72 = 74	2-2-18 = 22	3-3-8 = 14
1-2-36 = 39	2-3-12 = 17	3-4-6 = 13
1-3-24 = 28	2-4- 9 = 15	
1-4-18 = 23	2-6- 6 = 14	
1-6-12 = 19		
1-8- 9 = 18		

Since there was still a question after seeing the sum of the ages (the house number), there had to be more than one set of factors whose sum equaled this number (3-3-8 and 2-6-6). Since 2-6-6 does not yield an "oldest child" but 3-3-8 does, the ages of the children must have been 3, 3, and 8.

PROBLEM 34

The sum of two numbers is 2, and the product of these same numbers is 3. Find the sum of their reciprocals.

Discussion

The usual algebraic solution to this problem is as follows: Let x and y represent the two numbers. Then

$$x + y = 2$$
$$xy = 3$$

This yields a solution set

$$\left\{ \begin{matrix} x/x = 1 + i\sqrt{2} \\ y/y = 1 - i\sqrt{2} \end{matrix} \right\}$$

Now we must sum the reciprocals:

$$\frac{1}{1 + i\sqrt{2}} + \frac{1}{1 - i\sqrt{2}} = \frac{(1 - i\sqrt{2}) + (1 + i\sqrt{2})}{(1 + i\sqrt{2})(1 - i\sqrt{2})} = \frac{2}{3}$$

However, there is a more artistic solution. The sum of the reciprocals of x and y is given by the expression

$$\frac{1}{x} + \frac{1}{y} = \frac{x + y}{xy} = \frac{2}{3}$$

PROBLEM 35

A bridge that spans a bay is 1 mile long and is suspended from two supports, one at each end. As a result, when it expands a total of 2 feet from the summer heat, it "buckles" in the center, causing a bulge. How high is the bulge?

Discussion Draw a diagram of the bridge, both before and after the expansion causes it to buckle. (See Figure B-4.)

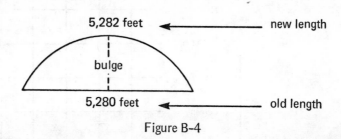

Figure B-4

We can now approximate the situation, using a diagram with two right triangles, as in Figure B-5.

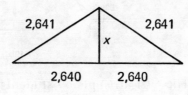

Figure B-5

The Pythagorean Theorem can now be applied to the right triangle:

$$x^2 + (2,640)^2 = (2,641)^2$$
$$x^2 + 6,969,600 = 6,974,881$$
$$x^2 = 5,281$$
$$x = 72.67$$

Thus the bulge is approximately 73 feet high.

*PROBLEM 36 A map of a local town is shown in Figure B-6. Billy lives at the corner of 4th Street and Fairfield Avenue. Betty lives at the corner of 8th Street and Appleton Avenue. Billy decides that he will visit Betty once a day after school until he has tried every different route to her house. Billy agrees to travel only east and north. How many different routes can Billy take to get to Betty's house?

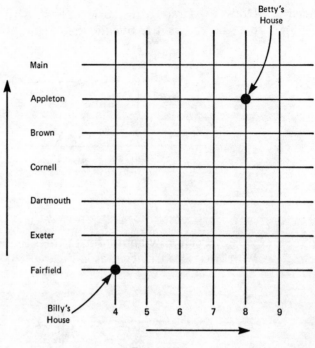

Figure B-6

Discussion   The first attempts by students to solve this problem usually involve trying to draw and count all of the different routes. This procedure is extremely cumbersome. It is easier to consider the number of different routes to each point on the grid in Figure B-7.

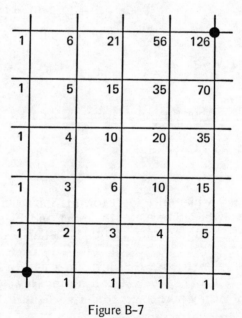

Figure B-7

100

A Collection of Non-Routine Problems

Notice that the numbers on the grid form the Pascal Triangle in Figure B–8.

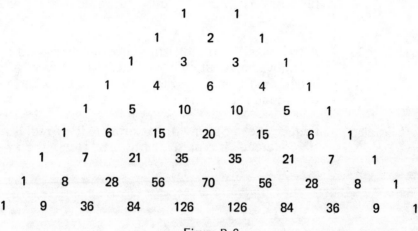

Figure B–8

*PROBLEM 37   An interesting variation on problem 36 is the following. Suppose we limit the direction of movement along the streets to that shown by the arrows in Figure B–9. How many different routes are there now from point A to point L?

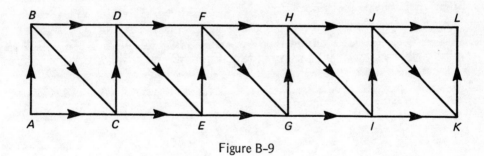

Figure B–9

Discussion   If we again examine the number of possible routes to each of the different points on the grid, we find another interesting series of numbers. (See Figure B–10.)

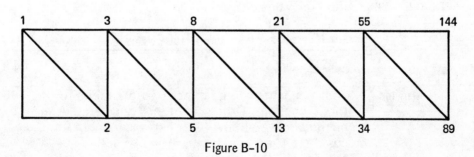

Figure B–10

The series 1, 2, 3, 5, 8, 13, 21, 34, 55, 89, 144, ... is the Fibonacci sequence of numbers—that is, each term after the first two is derived by adding the preceding two terms of the series. There are 144 different routes from A to L.

*PROBLEM 38

A steel band is fitted tightly around the equator. The band is removed and cut, and an additional 10 feet is added. The band now fits more loosely than it did before. How high off the ground is the band?

Discussion

Reduce the problem to that of a circle of radius r. Thus its circumference is represented by $2\pi r$. Now, when we increase

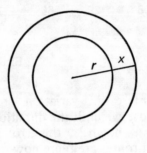

Figure B-11

the circumference by 10 feet, we increase the radius of the steel band by x. (See Figure B-11.) Thus,

$$2\pi(r + x) = 2\pi r + 10$$
$$2\pi r + 2\pi x = 2\pi r + 10$$
$$2\pi x = 10$$
$$x = \frac{10}{2\pi}$$

Therefore the steel band now fits approximately 1.6 feet above the surface of the earth.

PROBLEM 39

Find the value of

sin 10°	cos 10°	tan 10°	csc 10°	sec 10°	cot 10°
sin 20°	cos 20°	tan 20°	csc 20°	sec 20°	cot 20°

Discussion

Some students will go directly to the tables for the values of these functions. Others will use a calculator. A more elegant method of solution is to realize that $\sin x° \csc x° = 1$, $\cos x° \sec x° = 1$, and $\tan x° \cot x° = 1$. Thus the fraction reduces to 1/1 or simply 1.

PROBLEM 40   A cake in the form of a cube falls into a large vat of frosting and comes out frosted on all 6 faces. The cake is then cut into smaller cubes, each 1 inch on an edge. The cake is cut so that the number of pieces with frosting on 3 faces will be 1/8 the number of pieces having no frosting at all. We wish to have exactly enough pieces of cake for everyone. How many people will receive pieces of cake with frosting on exactly 3 faces? On exactly 2 faces? On exactly 1 face? On no faces? How large was the original cake?

Discussion   Make a table for a cube cake that originally was a $2 \times 2 \times 2$ cake, a $3 \times 3 \times 3$ cake, etc. Look for a pattern.

Cube	3 frosted faces	2 frosted faces	1 frosted faces	0 frosted faces	
$2 \times 2 \times 2$	8	0	0	0	= 8
$3 \times 3 \times 3$	8	12	6	1	= 27
$4 \times 4 \times 4$	8	24	24	8	= 64
$5 \times 5 \times 5$	8	36	54	27	= 125
$6 \times 6 \times 6$	8	48	96	64	= 216

Notice that the number of small cubes with exactly 3 frosted faces is *always* 8. Thus the cube we are looking for is the cube having 8 times as many no-frosting faces, or 64. This is the $6 \times 6 \times 6$ cube, as shown on our chart. Thus there are 48 cubes with frosting on exactly 2 faces, 96 cubes with frosting on exactly 1 face, and a total of 216 small cubes in all. The original cake must have been a $6 \times 6 \times 6$ cube.

PROBLEM 41   A commuter is in the habit of arriving at his suburban station each evening at exactly 6:00 P.M. His wife is always waiting for him with the car; she too arrives at exactly 6:00 P.M. She never varies her route or her rate of speed. One day he takes an earlier train, arriving at the station at 5:00 P.M. He decides not to call his wife, but begins to walk toward home along the route she always takes. They meet somewhere along the route, he gets into the car, and they drive home. They arrive home 10 minutes earlier than usual. How long had the husband been walking when he was picked up by his wife?

Discussion   If we pursue the problem from the point of view of the husband's time, we cannot arrive at an answer easily. So consider the problem from the point of view of the wife—i.e., how long she is gone from the house. Since they arrive home a total of 10 minutes earlier than usual, the car was gone a total of 5 minutes less in each direction. Thus the husband had been walking a total of 55 minutes when he was picked up.

PROBLEM 42   A woman was 3/8 of the way across a bridge when she heard the Wabash Cannonball Express approaching the bridge at 60 miles per hour. She quickly calculated that she could *just* save herself by running to either end of the bridge at top speed. How fast could she run?

Discussion   Draw a diagram, as in Figure B-12. We see that there are two different situations to consider.

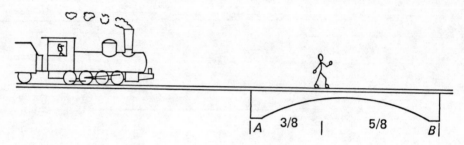

Figure B-12

If she can just get to either end of the bridge before the train arrives at that end, let her run away from the train toward point *B*. When the train arrives at point *A*, she will have covered an additional 3/8 of the bridge's length, or 3/4 of the bridge. She can now run the remaining 1/4 in the same time it will take the train to cover the entire 4/4 of the bridge. Thus her rate is 1/4 of that of the train, or 15 miles per hour.

Notice that a more formal algebraic solution can also be used. Let the bridge be 8 units of length, for example. Let x represent the distance the train is from point *A;* let y represent the woman's rate. Then we obtain the following two equations:

$$\frac{3}{y} = \frac{x}{60} \text{ (if the woman runs toward point } A)$$

$$\frac{5}{y} = \frac{x+8}{60} \text{ (if the woman runs toward point } B)$$

from which we get $y = 15$.

*PROBLEM 43 Ed and Dave were walking when they saw three people coming toward them. "I wonder how old they are," said Ed. Dave replied, "I know them! The product of their ages is 2,450, and the sum of their ages is twice your age." "That's all well and good," said Ed, "but I need some more information." "Oh, yes," agreed Dave. "Well, I'm older than any of the three." "Now I can figure their ages," said Ed.

Discussion We need to look at all the combinations of three factors whose product is 2,450.

5-14-35 (sum 54)	5-10-49 (sum 64)
10-35- 7 (sum 52)	2-25-49 (sum 76)
5- 5-28 (sum 38)	7-14-25 (sum 46)
7- 7-50 (sum 64)	7- 5-70 (sum 82)

Notice that there are others, but the factors could not represent ages under normal circumstances (e.g., 1-2-1,225, 1-10-245, etc.). Since the information "I am older than any of the three" is needed to provide a unique solution, Dave must be 50. If he were 51 or older, then both solutions whose sum equals 64 would be possible. Hence he must be 50, and the solution must be 49-10-5.

*PROBLEM 44 Two bicycle riders, Jeff and Nancy, are 25 miles apart, riding toward each other at speeds of 15 miles per hour and 10 miles per hour, respectively. A fly starts from Jeff and flies toward Nancy and then back to Jeff again and so on. The fly continues flying back and forth at a constant rate of 40 miles per hour, until the bicycle riders "collide" and crush the fly. How far has the fly traveled?

Discussion If we try to solve the problem using distance as our main focus, we arrive at a very complex series of equations. However, carefully examine the time it takes Jeff and Nancy to meet and crush the fly. Since they are moving toward each other at a constant rate of 25 miles per hour, it will take them only 1 hour of bicycling to reach each other. Thus the fly is moving back and forth for one hour, or a total of 40 miles.

PROBLEM 45 Two gentlemen were trying to decide when to open their store for business. "When the day after tomorrow is yesterday," said Marv, "then 'today' will be as far from Sunday as that day which was 'today' when the day before yesterday was tomorrow!" On which day of the week were the two men talking?

105

Discussion   Diagramming the conversation will lead us to discover that the men were talking on Sunday.

PROBLEM 46   The factory planners have built stations for their night watchmen at points A and B in Figure B–13. They are now ready to install check-in boxes along the two intersecting walls RS and TU. They wish to install these check-in boxes so that the watchmen walking from station A to the box on RS to the box on TU to station B will be making a minimum trip. What is the shortest path meeting these conditions?

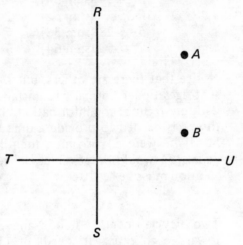

Figure B–13

Discussion   This problem requires a double reflection. We first reflect B through TU to point B'. (See Figure B–14.) Then we reflect B' through RS to B''. Now we draw AB'' to find the point for the check-in station along RS (point C). Then we draw CB' to find point D along TU.

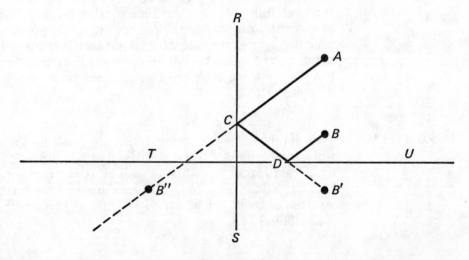

Figure B–14

106

PROBLEM 47   Lee must send one holiday gift out early this year. She doesn't know the exact amount of postage she will need to send it, but she does know it will be less than $3.19. She wants to buy as many stamps as necessary to make any combination up to $3.19. She could buy all 1¢ stamps, but that many might not fit on the package. What is the minimum number of stamps Lee should buy?

Discussion   We can take one-half the amount (rounding off to the next highest amount). This, together with stamps that make up the remaining one-half, will enable Lee to make any combination. We now repeat this procedure, always taking one-half the remainder. Thus we get Figure B–15.

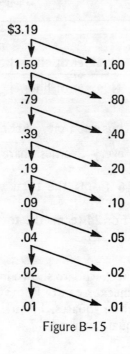

Figure B-15

If Lee buys stamps of 1¢, 1¢, 2¢, 5¢, 10¢, 20¢, 40¢, 80¢, and $1.60, she will be able to make any combination up to and including $3.19. Notice that this is not a unique solution; she could buy other combinations also containing 9 stamps (for example, 1¢, 1¢, 2¢, 4¢, 9¢, 19¢, 39¢, 79¢, and $1.65).

PROBLEM 48   There are 16 football teams in the National Football League. To conduct their annual draft, teams in each city must have a direct telephone line to each of the other cities. How many direct telephone lines must be installed by the telephone company to accomplish this? Suppose the league expands to 24 teams?

Discussion   Examine the problem using smaller numbers. We can start the

107

search for a pattern by using 1 city, 2 cities, 3 cities, etc. (See Figure B-16.)

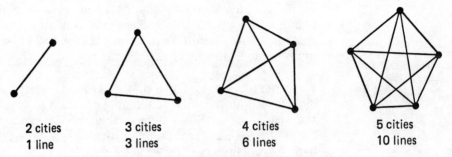

| 2 cities | 3 cities | 4 cities | 5 cities |
| 1 line | 3 lines | 6 lines | 10 lines |

Figure B-16

Number of cities	1	2	3	4	5	...	n
Number of lines	0	1	3	6	10	...	

Thus each city is connected to every other $(n - 1)$ city. Since every 2 cities share a line, our total will be $\frac{n(n - 1)}{2}$. For 16 teams the total will be $\frac{(16)(15)}{2}$ or 120 telephone lines. For 24 teams the total will be $\frac{(24)(23)}{2}$ or 276 lines.

*PROBLEM 49   The checkerboard shown in Figure B-17 contains one checker. The checker can only move diagonally "up" the board along the white squares. In how many ways can this checker reach the square marked A?

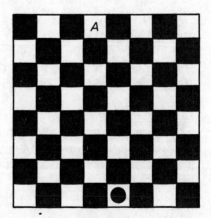

Figure B-17

108

Discussion   In Figure B–18 we have marked the number of ways the checker can reach each given square. For example, to reach the square labeled *B*, the checker might take exactly 3 different paths. Notice that these numbers form the Pascal Triangle, and thus we can compute that there are a total of 35 different paths the checker might take.

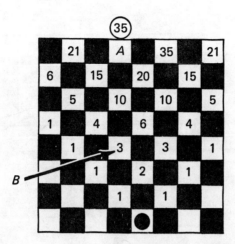

Figure B-18

PROBLEM 50   Mr. Lopez, who is 6 feet tall, wants to install a mirror on his bedroom wall that will enable him to see a full view of himself. What is the minimum-length mirror that will serve his needs, and how should it be placed on his wall?

Discussion   This interesting problem is resolved by applying a well-known theorem of geometry. A drawing, such as the one in Figure B–19, is the vital solution strategy.

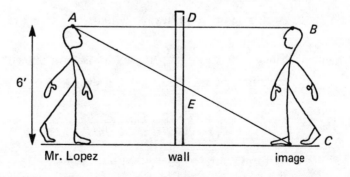

Figure B-19

Since the object, the image, and the wall are each perpendicular to the floor, the lines are parallel. Thus triangle

109

ABC has segment *DE* parallel to *BC* and equal in length to half of *BC*. The conclusion is that the mirror must be 3 feet in length and hung so that its lower edge is 3 feet from the floor. Notice how Figure B-20 shows that the distance Mr. Lopez stands from the mirror does not affect the answer.

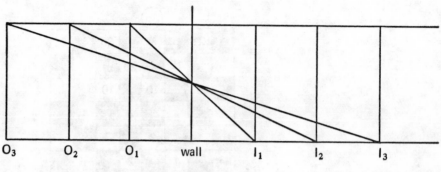

O_3 $\qquad$ O_2 $\qquad$ O_1 $\qquad$ wall $\qquad$ I_1 $\qquad$ I_2 $\qquad$ I_3

Figure B-20

PROBLEM 51   Irwin insists on adding two fractions by adding their numerators and then adding their denominators. Thus, when adding 9/12 and −1/4, Irwin gets

$$\frac{9 + -1}{12 + \ 4} = \frac{8}{16} = \frac{1}{2}$$

To show his method is correct, Irwin adds 9/12 and −1/4 in the usual manner and gets

$$\frac{9 + -3}{12} = \frac{6}{12} = \frac{1}{2}$$

Are there other values for which $\frac{a}{b} + \frac{c}{d} = \frac{a+c}{b+d}$?

Discussion   Since $\frac{a}{b} + \frac{c}{d} = \frac{a+c}{b+d}$ merely adds symbols with no regard for meaning, we wish to find values for which

$$\frac{a}{b} + \frac{c}{d} = \frac{ad + bc}{bd} = \frac{a+c}{b+d}$$

Performing the algebra, we obtain $(ad + bc)(b + d) = bd(a + c)$, and finally $c = -\frac{ad^2}{b^2}$, where b and $d \neq 0$. Integral values of a, b, c, and d that satisfy the above relationship will yield fractions to which Irwin's method may be applied.

110

PROBLEM 52   The Appletree Garden Service must plant 69,489 apple trees in the 9 days before winter sets in. Every day after the first, the foreman puts 6 additional men on the job. However, every day after the first, each man plants 5 fewer trees than each did on the previous day. As a result, the number of trees planted per man keeps going down each day. What was the largest number of trees planted on any one day?

Discussion   If we let the number of men working on the middle (the fifth) day be m, and the number of trees planted on that day be n, then mn trees were planted on the fifth day. On the fourth day, there were $(m - 6)(n + 5)$ trees planted; on the sixth day, there were $(m + 6)(n - 5)$ trees planted; and so on. Thus the totals for the 9 days would be $9mn - 1,800 = 69,489$, or $mn = 7,921$. Now 7,921 is the square of 89 (a prime number). Hence the chart of the work done would be

Day 1	65 men × 109 trees = 7,085
Day 2	71 men × 104 trees = 7,384
Day 3	77 men × 99 trees = 7,623
Day 4	83 men × 94 trees = 7,802
Day 5	89 men × 89 trees = 7,921
Day 6	95 men × 84 trees = 7,980
Day 7	101 men × 79 trees = 7,979
Day 8	107 men × 74 trees = 7,918
Day 9	113 men × 69 trees = 7,797
	69,489

The largest number of trees planted on any one day was 7,980 trees on the sixth day.

*PROBLEM 53   In a game called crossball, a team can score either 3 points or 7 points. Which scores can a team *not* make?

Discussion   We set up a table to organize our discussion:

Not possible	1	2		4	5			8			11				
Possible			3			6	7		9	10		12	13	14	15	...

Apparently a team can make every score after 11.

Notice that we can extend this problem as follows: Given any two relatively prime numbers, what is the greatest counting number that cannot be expressed using these numbers either singly, repeatedly, in addition, or in combination? (This leads to the formula $ab - (a + b)$ as the method for determining the answer.)

PROBLEM 54   Three cylindrical oil drums of 2-foot diameter are to be securely fastened in the form of a "triangle" by a steel band. What length of band will be required?

Discussion   The careful drawing of the situation in Figure B-21 is the fundamental strategy used here.

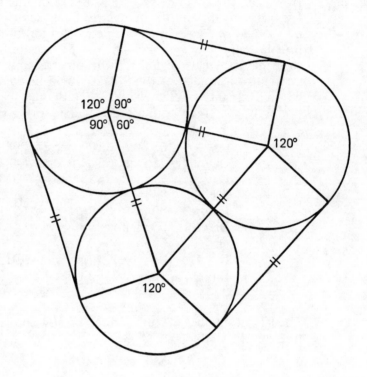

Figure B-21

Notice that the band consists of three straight sections (tangents) and three curved sections (arcs). The straight sections form rectangles with the line of centers, and thus each equals $2r$ or 2 feet. The curved sections are each arcs whose central angle is 120°, and thus each arc is 1/3 of a circle, or $(1/3)\,(\pi d)$. The total length is

$$3(2) + 3(\frac{1}{3}\pi d) = 6 + \pi d$$

Since $d = 2$ feet, the length of the steel band will be $6 + 2\pi$ feet, or approximately 12.28 feet.

Notice that this problem can be generalized for n barrels and also extended to barrels of different diameters.

112

PROBLEM 55   A high school geometry class was given the problem of find-
ing the height of the flagpole in the school yard with only a
mirror and a measuring tape. Several of the students successfully answered the question. How did they solve the
problem?

Discussion   Draw a diagram of the situation, as in Figure B–22.

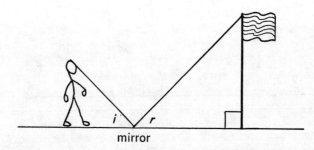

mirror

Figure B–22

Since the two triangles are similar (the angle of incidence i
equals the angle of reflection r), a simple proportion reveals
the answer.

A
Bibliography of
Problem-Solving
Resources

A Bibliography of Problem-Solving Resources

1. Adler, Irving. *Magic House of Numbers.* John Day Company, New York, New York, 1974.
2. *Arithmetic Teacher.* The entire November 1977 issue is devoted to problem solving. National Council of Teachers of Mathematics, Reston, Virginia.
3. Ball, W. W. R. *Mathematical Recreations and Essays* (12th edition, revised by H. S. M. Coxeter). Reprinted by University of Toronto Press, Toronto, Ontario, 1974.
4. Barnard, Douglas. *A Book of Mathematical and Reasoning Problems.* D. Van Nostrand Company, New York, New York, 1962.
5. Butts, Thomas. *Problem Solving in Mathematics.* Scott, Foresman and Company, Glenview, Illinois, 1973.
6. Charosh, Mannis (editor). *Mathematical Challenges.* National Council of Teachers of Mathematics, Reston, Virginia, 1973.
7. Dodson, J. *Characteristics of Successful Insightful Problem Solvers.* University Microfilm, Number 71-13, 048, Ann Arbor, Michigan, 1970.
8. Dudeney, H. E. *Amusements in Mathematics.* Dover Publishing Company, New York, New York, 1958.
9. *Enrichment for the Grades,* Twenty-seventh yearbook. National Council of Teachers of Mathematics, Reston, Virginia, 1966-1971.
10. Fixx, James. *Games for the Superintelligent.* Doubleday and Company, Garden City, New York, 1972.
11. Frolichstein, Jack. *Mathematical Fun, Games and Puzzles.* Dover Publishing Company, New York, New York, 1967.
12. Gardner, Martin. *Aha!* Scientific American/W. H. Freeman and Company, San Francisco, California, 1978.
13. ———. *Scientific American Book of Mathematical Puzzles and Diversions.* Simon and Schuster, New York, New York, 1959.
14. ———. *Second Scientific American Book of Mathematical Puzzles and Diversions.* Simon and Schuster, New York, New York, 1961.
15. ——— (editor). *Mathematic Puzzles of Sam Lloyd.* Simon and Schuster, New York, New York, 1959.
16. ——— (editor). *More Mathematical Puzzles of Sam Lloyd.* Simon and Schuster, New York, New York, 1960.
17. Greenes, Carole; Gregory, John; and Seymour, Dale. *Successful Problem Solving Techniques.* Creative Publications, Palo Alto, California, 1978.
18. ———; Spungin, Rika; and Dombrowski, Justine M. *Problem-Matics.* Creative Publications, Palo Alto, California, 1978.
19. Heafford, Philip. *The Math Entertainer.* Harper & Row, Publishers, New York, New York, 1973.
20. Jacoby, Oswald, and Benson, William H. *Mathematics for Pleasure.* Fawcett World Library, New York, New York, 1965.
21. Kaufman, Gerald L. *The Book of Modern Puzzles.* Dover Publishing Company, New York, New York, 1954.
22. Kordemsky, Boris A. *The Moscow Puzzles.* Charles Scribner's Sons, New York, New York, 1972.
23. Kraitchik, Maurice. *Mathematical Recreations* (2nd edition). Dover Publishing Company, New York, New York, 1953.
24. Longley-Cook, L. H. *New Math Puzzle Book.* Van Nostrand Reinhold Company, New York, New York, 1970.
25. May, Francis B. *Introduction to Games of Strategy.* Allyn and Bacon, Boston, Massachusetts, 1970.

26. Mira, Julio. *Mathematical Teasers.* Barnes and Noble, New York, New York, 1970.
27. Mott-Smith, Geoffrey. *Mathematical Puzzles for Beginners and Enthusiasts* (2nd edition). Dover Publishing Company, New York, New York, 1954.
28. Peck, Lyman. *Secret Codes, Remainder Arithmetic, and Matrices.* National Council of Teachers of Mathematics, Reston, Virginia, 1961.
29. Polya, George. *How to Solve It.* Princeton University Press, Princeton, New Jersey, 1971.
30. ———. *Mathematical Discovery: On Understanding, Learning and Teaching Problem Solving* (two volumes). John Wiley and Sons, New York, New York (Volume 1) 1962, (Volume 2) 1965.
31. ———, and Kilpatrick, Jeremy. *The Stanford Mathematics Problem Book.* Teachers College Press, New York, New York, 1974.
32. *Problematical Recreations.* A series of small pamphlets containing puzzles and problems. Litton Industries, Inc., Beverly Hills, California.
33. Rademacher, Hans, and Toeplitz, Otto. *The Enjoyment of Mathematics.* Princeton University Press, Princeton, New Jersey, 1957.
34. Ranucci, Ernest. *Puzzles, Problems, Posers, and Pastimes* (three volumes). Houghton Mifflin Company, Boston, Massachusetts, 1972.
35. Salkind, Charles T. *The Contest Problem Book* (two volumes). Mathematical Association of America, Washington, D.C., 1975.
36. Schaaf, William. *A Bibliography of Recreational Mathematics* (four volumes). National Council of Teachers of Mathematics, Reston, Virginia (Volume 1) 1970, (Volume 2) 1970, (Volume 3) 1973, (Volume 4) 1978.
37. *School Science and Mathematics.* The entire March 1978 issue is devoted to problem solving. School Science and Mathematics Association, Inc., Kalamazoo, Michigan.
38. Shklarsky, D. O.; Chentzov, N. N.; and Yaglom, I. M. *The U.S.S.R. Olympiad Problem Book.* W. H. Freeman and Company, San Francisco, California, 1962.
39. Trigg, C. W. *Mathematical Quickies.* McGraw-Hill Book Company, New York, New York, 1967.
40. Wickelgren, Wayne. *How to Solve Problems.* W. H. Freeman and Company, San Francisco, California, 1974.
41. Williams, J. D. *The Compleat Strategyst* (rev. ed.). McGraw-Hill Book Company, New York, New York, 1965.
42. Wylie, C. R. *One Hundred One Puzzles in Thought and Logic.* Dover Publishing Company, New York, New York, 1957.

SECTION D

Masters
for
Selected
Problems

The following problems are from Chapters 1, 2, and 3:
1. Locker problem on page 7
2. Handshake problem on page 9
3. Checkerboard problem on page 10
4. Calculator problem on page 22
5. Card game problem on page 39
6. Scale problem on page 43
7. Pirate problem on page 49
8. Triangle problem on page 51
9. Hamburger problem on page 56
10. Billiard ball problem on page 60

The following problems are from Section B:
11. #4
12. #5
13. #10
14. #18
15. #29
16. #31
17. #32
18. #33
19. #35
20. #36
21. #40
22. #44
23. #48
24. #50
25. #54

Problem: The new school has exactly 1,000 lockers and exactly 1,000 students. On the first day of school, the students meet outside the building and agree on the following plan: The first student will enter the school and open all of the lockers. The second student will then enter the school and close every locker with an even number (2, 4, 6, 8, . . .). The third student will then "reverse" every third locker. That is, if the locker is closed, he will open it; if the locker is open, he will close it. The fourth student will reverse every fourth locker, and so on until all 1,000 students in turn have entered the building and reversed the proper lockers. Which lockers will finally remain open?

NAME _____   DATE _____

Problem: There are eight people in a room. Each person shakes hands with each of the other people once and only once. How many handshakes are there?

Problem: How many squares are there on a standard checkerboard?

Problem: The 7 and 8 keys on my calculator don't work. How might I find the sum of 274 + 882 + 1,028?

Problem: A, B, and C decide to play a game of cards. They agree on the following procedure: When a player loses a game, he or she will double the amount of money that each of the other players already has. First A loses a hand and doubles the amount of money that B and C each have. Then B loses a hand and doubles the amount of money that A and C each have. Then C loses a hand and doubles the amount of money that A and B each have. The three players then decide to quit, and they find that each player now has $8. Who was the biggest loser?

Problem: Three boys stood on a scale and put a nickel in the slot. The scale showed 390 pounds as their total weight. One boy stepped off the scale. It then showed 255 pounds. The second boy stepped off the scale, and it then showed 145 pounds. Find the weights of all three boys.

133

Problem: A pirate ship at point A in the diagram shown is 50 meters directly north of point C on the shore. Point D, also on the shore and due east of point C, is 130 meters from point C. Point B, a lighthouse, is due north of point D and 80 meters from point D. The pirate ship must touch the shoreline and then sail to the lighthouse. Find the location of point X on the shoreline, so that the path from A to X to B will be a minimum.

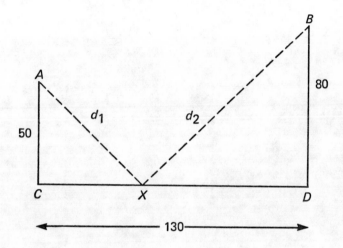

Problem: How many triangles can you find in this figure?

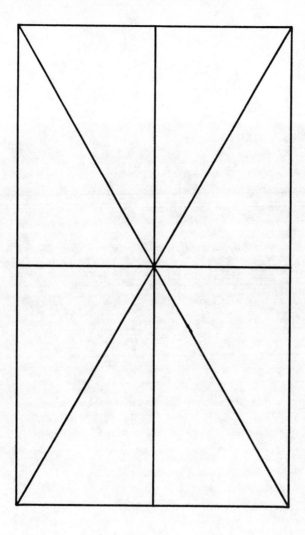

137

Problem: A major hamburger chain has sold 22 billion hamburgers, each 1 inch thick. If we stacked these hamburgers, how many miles high would the stack be?

NAME _____ DATE _____

Problem: Three boxes each contain a number of billiard balls. One box contains only even-numbered billiard balls, one box contains only odd-numbered billiard balls, and the third box contains a mixture of odd- and even-numbered billiard balls. *All* of the boxes are mislabeled. By selecting one ball from one of the boxes, can you correctly label the three boxes? Why or why not?

NAME _____ DATE _____

Problem: A grocer has three pails: an empty pail that holds 5 liters, an empty pail that holds 3 liters, and an 8-liter pail that is filled with apple cider. Show how the grocer can measure exactly 4 liters of apple cider with the help of the 5-liter and 3-liter pails.

Problem: In how many different ways can three people divide 25 pieces of candy so that each person gets at least 1 piece?

Problem: A woman has some cows and some chickens. Together the animals have a total of 54 legs. How many cows and how many chickens might she have?

Problem: Luisa was playing darts. She threw 6 darts, and all 6 hit the target shown. Which of the following could be her score?

4, 17, 56. 28, 29, 31

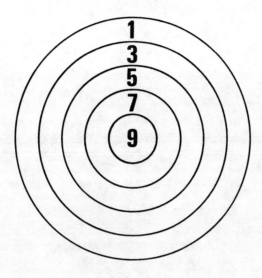

Problem: A textbook is opened at random. To what pages is it opened if the product of the facing page numbers is 3,192?

Problem: The following advertisement appeared in the real estate section of a local newspaper:

INVESTMENT FOR THE FUTURE!
LAND FOR SALE—
ONLY 5¢ PER SQUARE INCH!!

Invest your money now in land,
in an area that is soon to be developed.
For information, call or write

Land Developers, Inc.

If you were to buy an acre of land as advertised, what amount would you be required to pay?

Problem: The probability of rolling a 2 on a standard pair of dice is 1/36; the probability of rolling a 3 is 2/36 (a 1-2 or a 2-1); and so on. How could you re-mark a pair of dice so that the probability of throwing each number from 1 through 12 was the same?

155

Problem: During the recent census, a man told the census-taker that he had three children. When asked their ages, he replied, "The product of their ages is 72. The sum of their ages is the same as my house number." The census-taker ran to the door and looked at the house number. "I still can't tell," she complained. The man replied, "Oh, that's right. I forgot to tell you that the oldest one likes chocolate pudding." The census-taker promptly wrote down the ages of the three children. How old are they?

Problem: A bridge that spans a bay is 1 mile long and is suspended from two supports, one at each end. As a result, when it expands a total of 2 feet from the summer heat, it "buckles" in the center, causing a bulge. How high is the bulge?

Problem: A map of a local town is shown in the figure below. Billy lives at the corner of 4th Street and Fairfield Avenue. Betty lives at the corner of 8th Street and Appleton Avenue. Billy decides that he will visit Betty once a day after school until he has tried every different route to her house. Billy agrees to travel only east and north. How many different routes can Billy take to get to Betty's house?

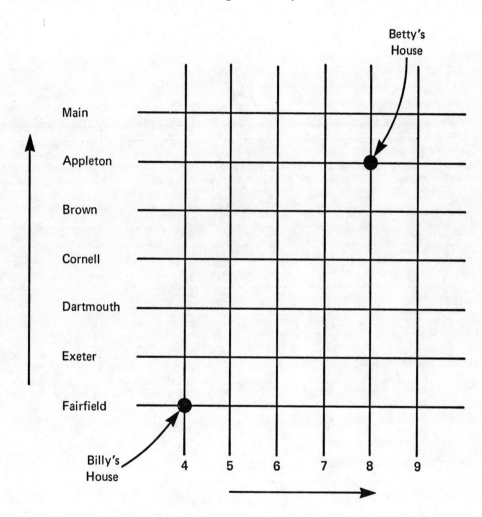

Problem: A cake in the form of a cube falls into a large vat of frosting and comes out frosted on all 6 faces. The cake is then cut into smaller cubes, each 1 inch on an edge. The cake is cut so that the number of pieces with frosting on 3 faces will be 1/8 the number of pieces having no frosting at all. We wish to have exactly enough pieces of cake for everyone. How many people will receive pieces of cake with frosting on exactly 3 faces? On exactly 2 faces? On exactly 1 face? On no faces? How large was the original cake?

Problem: Two bicycle riders, Jeff and Nancy, are 25 miles apart, riding toward each other at speeds of 15 miles per hour and 10 miles per hour, respectively. A fly starts from Jeff and flies toward Nancy and then back to Jeff again and so on. The fly continues flying back and forth at a constant rate of 40 miles per hour, until the bicycle riders "collide" and crush the fly. How far has the fly traveled?

40 miles per hour

Jeff ———— 15 miles *per* 5 miles ————→ 10 miles *per* Nancy

18 miles

Problem: There are 16 football teams in the National Football League. To conduct their annual draft, teams in each city must have a direct telephone line to each of the other cities. How many direct telephone lines must be installed by the telephone company to accomplish this? Suppose the league expands to 24 teams.

Problem: Mr. Lopez, who is 6 feet tall, wants to install a mirror on his bedroom wall that will enable him to see a full view of himself. What is the minimum-length mirror that will serve his needs, and how should it be placed on his wall?

Problem: Three cylindrical oil drums of 2-foot diameter are to be securely fastened in the form of a triangle by a steel band. What length of band will be required?

Masters
for
Strategy
Game
Boards

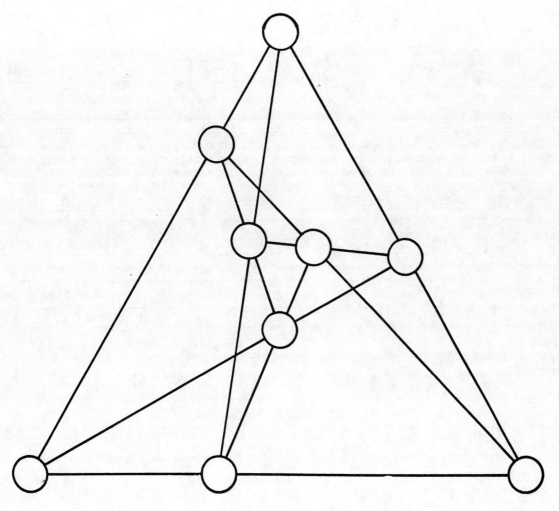

Triangular Tic-Tac-Toe

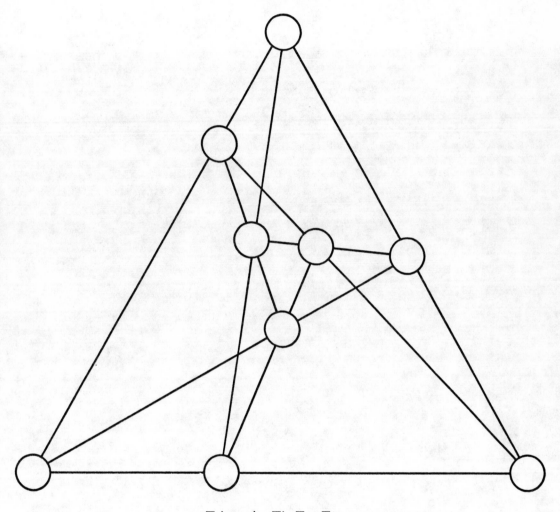

Triangular Tic-Tac-Toe

179

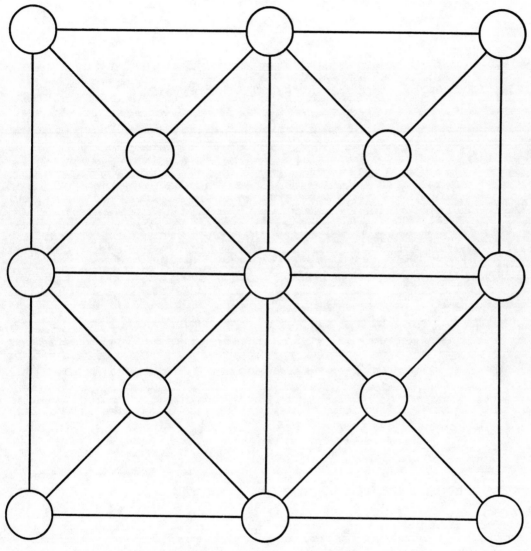

Put 'Em Down Tic-Tac-Toe

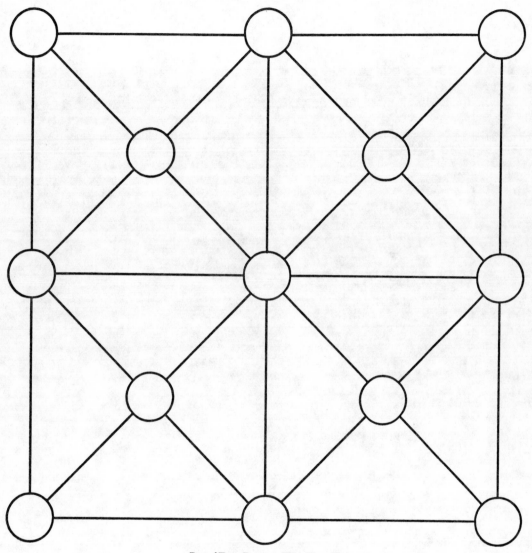

Put 'Em Down Tic-Tac-Toe

Point Score Tic-Tac-Toe

Point Score Tic-Tac-Toe

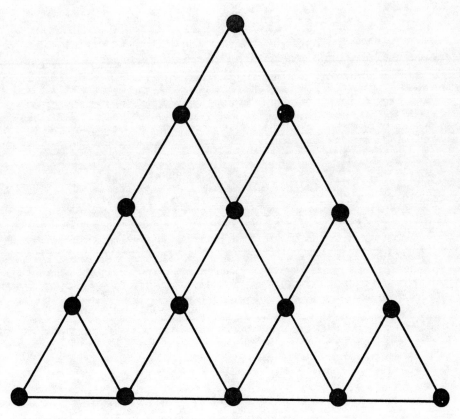

Dots-in-a-Row Tic-Tac-Toe

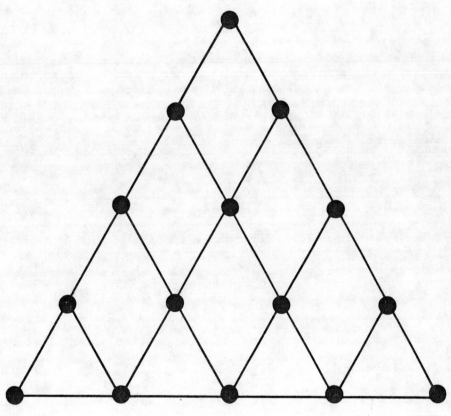

Dots-in-a-Row Tic-Tac-Toe

191

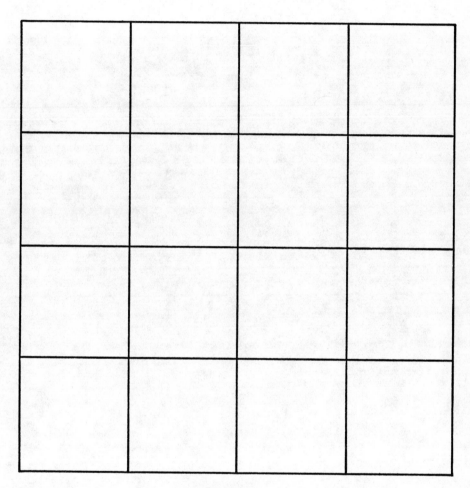

Tac-Tic-Toe

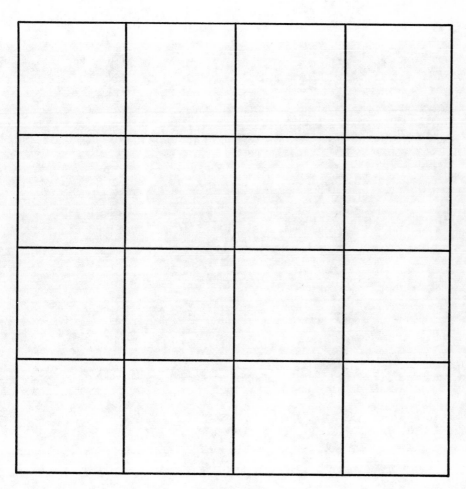

Tac-Tic-Toe

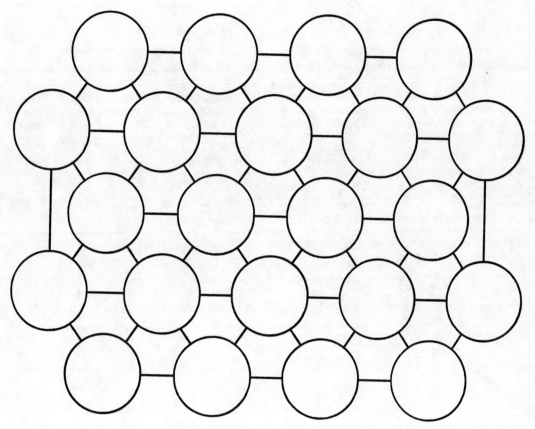

Tac-Tic-Toe, Chinese Version

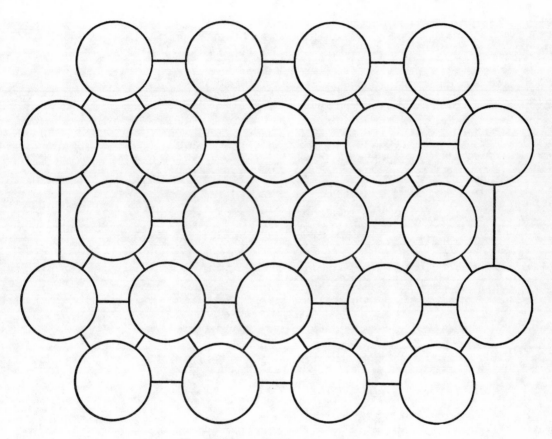

Tac-Tic-Toe, Chinese Version

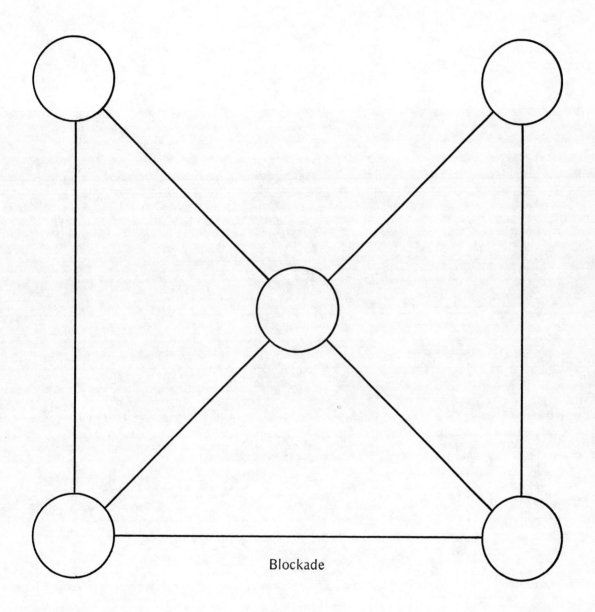

Blockade

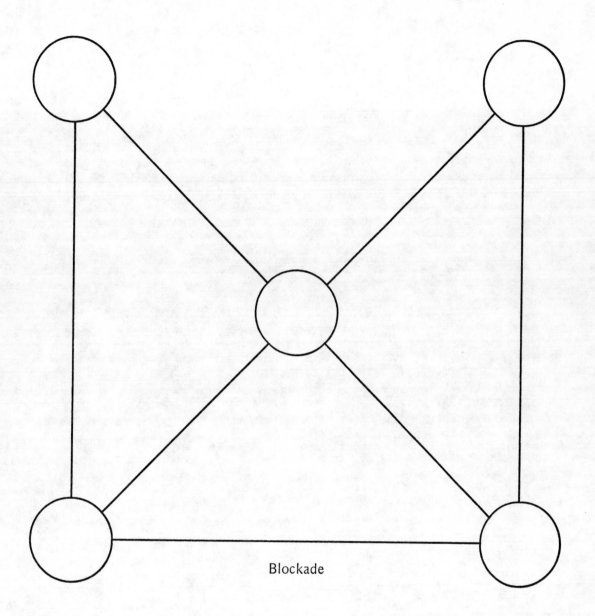

Blockade

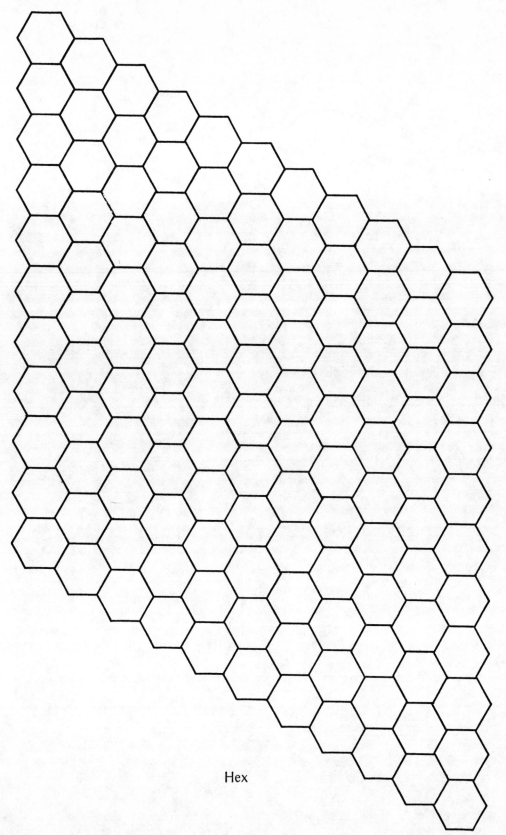

Hex

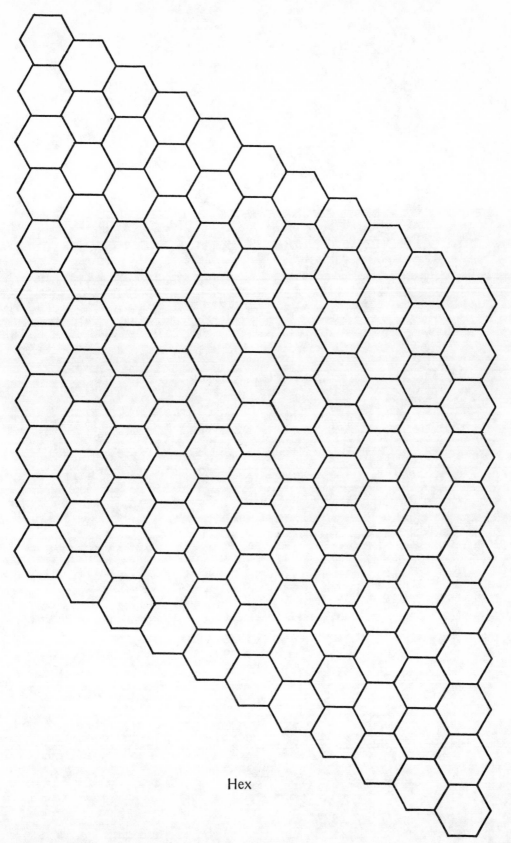

Hex

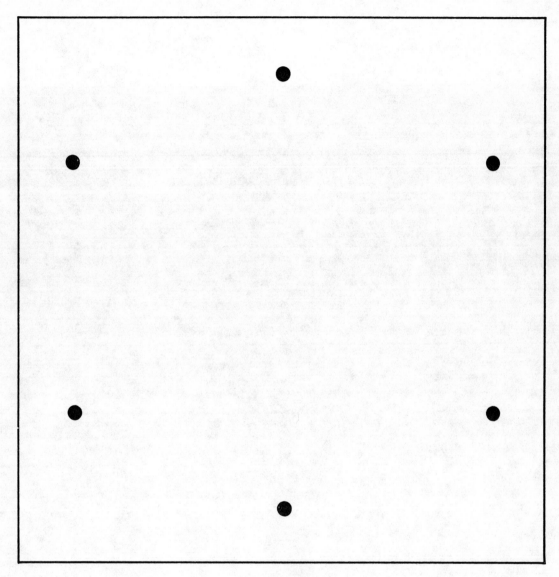

Triahex

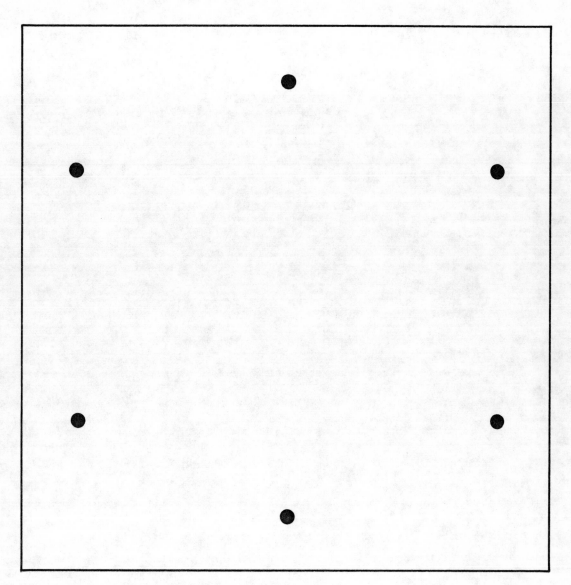

Triahex

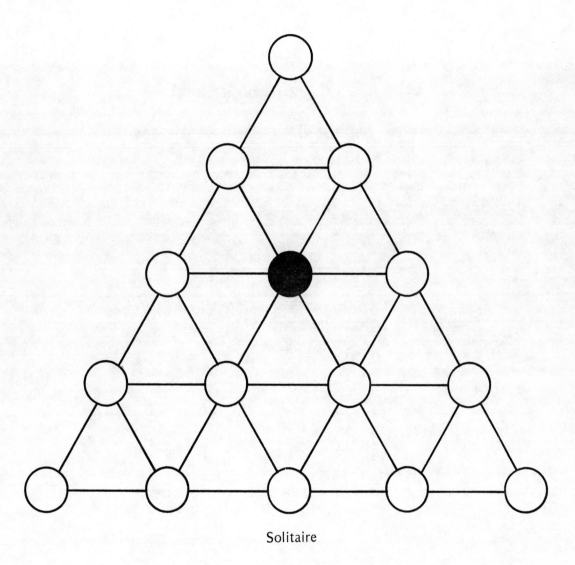

Solitaire

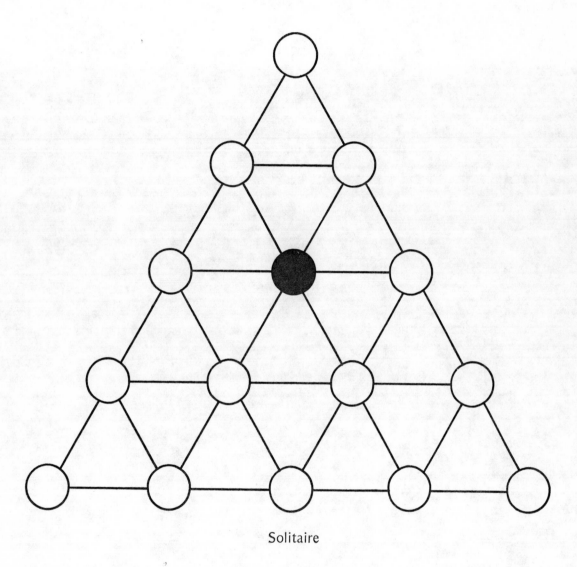

Solitaire

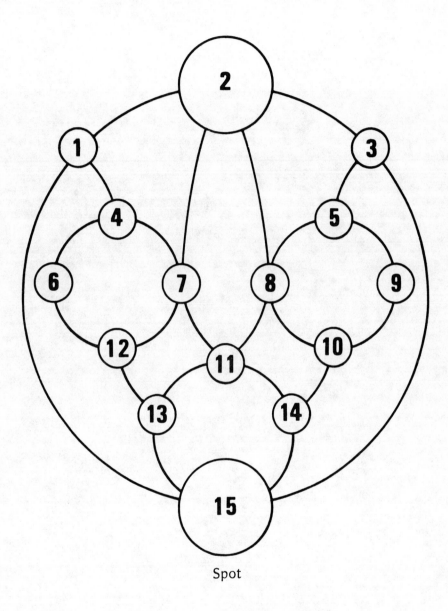

Spot

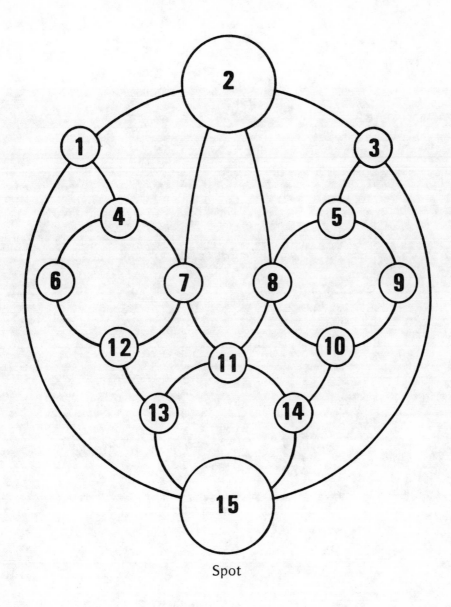

Spot

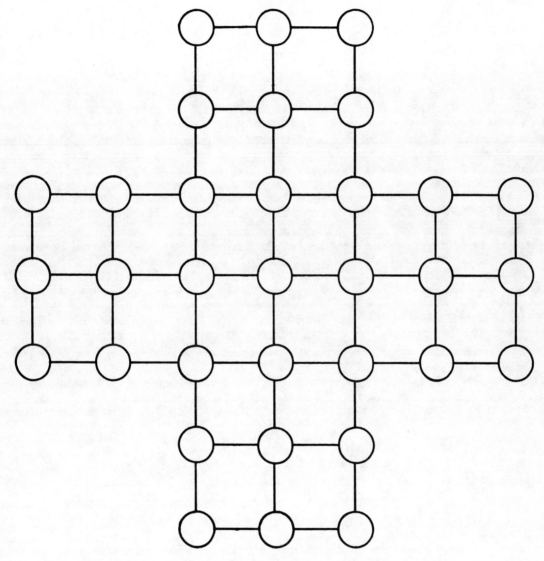

Fox and Geese

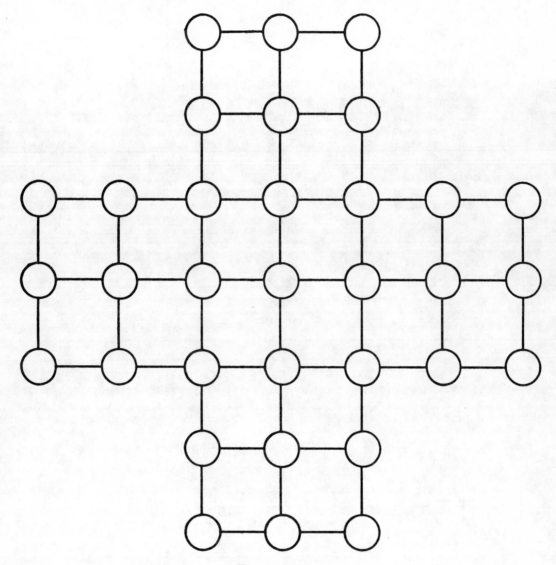

Fox and Geese

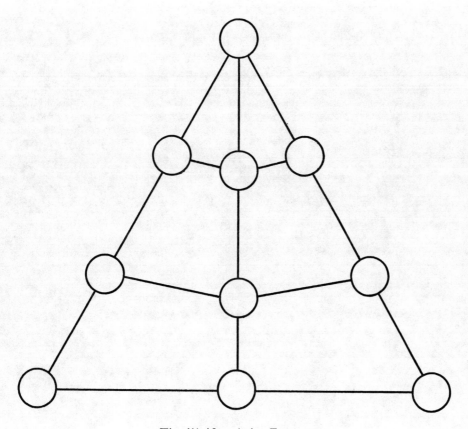

The Wolf and the Farmers

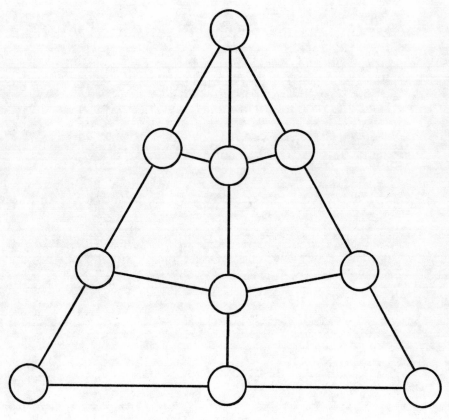

The Wolf and the Farmers